AIR FRYER RESTAURANT RECIPES

Publications International, Ltd.

Some of the products listed in this publication may be in limited distribution.

Pictured on the front cover (clockwise from top left): Crispy Mushrooms (page 10), Spinach Florentine Flatbread (page 86), Avocado Egg Rolls (page 28), Macaroni and Cheese Bites (page 16), and Air-Fried Beef Taquitos (page 119).

Pictured on the back cover (clockwise from top left): Ricotta Pancakes (page 47), Mozzarella Sticks (page 26), Chicken Air-Fried Steak with Creamy Gravy (page 142), Cheddar Biscuits (page 52), Chocolate-Orange Lava Cakes (page 178), and Shrimp and Spinach Salad (page 64).

Photograph on page 19 © Shutterstock.com.

ISBN: 978-1-63938-022-0

Manufactured in China.

8 7 6 5 4 3 2 1

Microwave Cooking: Microwave ovens vary in wattage. Use the cooking times as guidelines and check for doneness before adding more time.

Let's get social!
@Publications_International
@PublicationsInternational
www.pilbooks.com

CONTENTS

INTRODUCTION...4

APPETIZERS & STARTERS...6

BREAKFAST BITES...46

HEARTY SALADS...58

SANDWICHES & SMALL BITES...78

DINNER WINNERS...118

ON THE SIDE...154

SWEETS & TREATS...174

INDEX...187

TRADEMARKS...190

INTRODUCTION

Do you love those tasty iconic restaurant dishes? Would you like to be able to prepare your favorites at home and a bit healthier, too?

Your air fryer is your answer to preparing many of the delicious foods in your own kitchen without added fat or guilt. You'll get the foods you love and crave in the convenience of your own home. Plus, you'll soon see how your air fryer is so easy to use, cooks food faster and provides a no-fuss clean up.

You may have thought that your air fryer only prepares healthier "fried foods," but you'll soon find that you can prepare all types of other foods in it, too. Prepare everything from appetizers to meals to sides and even desserts! Why not try pizza or sandwiches? Maybe, a tasty chicken breast or marinated salmon to top your favorite salad or as a main dish? Or, how about a side of roasted vegetables? You'll soon realize how versatile your air fryer is—from baking to grilling, steaming, roasting, and reheating.

Choose from more than 90 of your favorite dishes here, or try to create your own. Once you learn how to use your air fryer, you'll realize how easy it is to master it.

Now, enjoy your favorite foods at home. Plus, as an added benefit, you'll have the recipes at your fingertips to prepare over and over again!

HELPFUL TIPS

- Read your air fryer's manufacturer's directions carefully before cooking to make sure you understand the specific features of your air fryer before starting to cook.

- Preheat your air fryer for 2 to 3 minutes before cooking.

- You can cook foods typically prepared in the oven in your air fryer. But because the air fryer is more condensed than a regular oven, it is recommended that recipes cut 25°F to 50°F off temperature and 20% off the typical cooking times.

- Avoid having foods stick to your air fryer basket by using nonstick cooking spray or cooking on parchment paper or foil. You can also get food to brown and crisp more easily by spraying occasionally with nonstick cooking spray during the cooking process.

- Don't overfill your basket. Each air fryer differs in its basket size. Cook foods in batches as needed.

- Use toothpicks to hold food in place. You may notice that light foods may blow around from the pressure of the fan. Just be sure to secure foods in the basket to prevent this.
- Check foods while cooking by opening the air fryer basket. This will not disturb cooking times. Once you return the basket, the cooking resumes.
- Experiment with cooking times of various foods. Test foods for doneness before consuming—check meats and poultry with a meat thermometer, and use a toothpick to test muffins and cupcakes.
- Use your air fryer to cook frozen foods, too! Frozen French fries, fish sticks, chicken nuggets, individual pizzas—these all work great. Just remember to reduce cooking temperatures and times.

ESTIMATED COOKING TEMPERATURES/TIMES*

FOOD	TEMPERATURE	TIMING
Vegetables (asparagus, broccoli, corn-on-the-cob, green beans, mushrooms, tomatoes)	390°F	6 to 10 min.
Vegetables (bell peppers, cauliflower, eggplant, onions, potatoes, zucchini)	390°F	10 to 15 min.
Chicken (bone-in)	370°F	20 to 25 min.
Chicken (boneless)	370°F	12 to 15 min.
Beef (ground beef)	370°F	15 to 17 min.
Beef (steaks, roasts)	390°F	10 to 15 min.
Pork	370°F	12 to 15 min.
Fish	390°F	10 to 12 min.
Frozen Foods	390°F	10 to 15 min.

This is just a guide. All food varies in size, weight, and texture. Be sure to test your food for preferred doneness before consuming it. Also, some foods will need to be shaken or flipped to help distribute ingredients for proper cooking.

Make note of the temperatures and times that work best for you for continued success of your air fryer.

Enjoy and have fun!

APPETIZERS & STARTERS

INSPIRED BY RED ROBIN® GOURMET BURGERS & BREWS
AIR-FRIED PARMESAN PICKLE CHIPS
MAKES 8 SERVINGS

4 large whole dill pickles
½ cup all-purpose flour
½ teaspoon salt
2 eggs

½ cup panko bread crumbs
2 tablespoons grated Parmesan cheese
½ cup garlic aioli mayonnaise or ranch dressing

1 Line baking sheet with paper towels. Slice pickles diagonally into ¼-inch slices; place on prepared baking sheet. Pat dry on top with paper towels to remove any moisture from pickles.

2 Combine flour and salt in shallow dish. Beat eggs in another shallow dish. Combine panko and Parmesan cheese in third shallow dish.

3 Coat pickles in flour. Dip in eggs, letting excess drip back into dish, then coat evenly with panko.

4 Preheat air fryer to 390°F. Cook in batches 8 to 10 minutes or until golden brown. Remove carefully. Serve with aioli or dressing.

BRUSCHETTA

MAKES 8 SERVINGS (1 CUP)

4 plum tomatoes, seeded and diced

½ cup packed fresh basil leaves, finely chopped

5 tablespoons olive oil, divided

2 cloves garlic, minced

2 teaspoons finely chopped oil-packed sun-dried tomatoes

¼ teaspoon salt

⅛ teaspoon black pepper

16 slices Italian bread

2 tablespoons grated Parmesan cheese

1 Combine fresh tomatoes, basil, 3 tablespoons oil, garlic, sun-dried tomatoes, salt and pepper in large bowl; mix well. Let stand at room temperature 1 hour to blend flavors.

2 Brush remaining 2 tablespoons oil over one side of bread slices; sprinkle with cheese.

3 Preheat air fryer to 350°F. Place bread in single layer in basket. Cook in batches 3 to 5 minutes or until toasted.

4 Top each bread slice with 1 tablespoon tomato mixture.

CRISPY MUSHROOMS

MAKES 4 SERVINGS

- ½ cup all-purpose flour
- ½ cup garlic and herb-flavored bread crumbs
- ½ cup grated Parmesan cheese
- ½ teaspoon paprika
- ½ teaspoon salt
- ¼ teaspoon black pepper
- 2 eggs
- 1 teaspoon water
- 1 package (8 ounces) whole mushrooms

GARLIC MAYONNAISE

- ½ cup mayonnaise
- 2 teaspoons minced garlic
- 1 teaspoon lemon juice
- Fresh chopped parsley (optional)

1 Combine flour, bread crumbs, Parmesan cheese, paprika, salt and pepper in medium bowl. Whisk egg and water in separate bowl.

2 Preheat air fryer to 370°F. Line basket with parchment paper.

3 Using a fork, dip mushrooms into egg mixture, allowing excess to drip back into bowl. Coat with bread crumb mixture, coating thoroughly. Spray mushrooms with nonstick cooking spray.

4 Cook in batches 6 to 8 minutes or until golden brown, spraying with cooking spray halfway though cooking.

5 Prepare Garlic Mayonnaise. Combine mayonnaise, garlic and lemon juice in small bowl; mix well. Sprinkle with parsley, if desired. Serve mushrooms with Garlic Mayonnaise.

ZESTY LEMON-PEPPER WINGS

MAKES 8 SERVINGS

2 pounds chicken drummettes
1 teaspoon garlic powder
1 teaspoon onion powder
1 teaspoon salt, divided
½ teaspoon paprika
⅓ cup all-purpose flour

½ teaspoon black pepper
¼ cup (½ stick) butter, melted
2 tablespoons lemon-pepper seasoning
1 teaspoon dried parsley flakes

1 Place chicken in large resealable food storage bag. Combine garlic powder, onion powder, ½ teaspoon salt and paprika in small bowl. Add to bag with chicken; toss well.

2 Combine flour, remaining ½ teaspoon salt and black pepper in shallow bowl. Remove chicken from bag; roll lightly in flour mixture.

3 Preheat air fryer to 370°F. Line basket with foil.

4 Add chicken to basket in single layer. Spray lightly with nonstick cooking spray. Cook 15 to 18 minutes, flipping halfway through cooking and spraying with cooking spray, until chicken is golden brown. Remove to serving bowl.

5 Combine melted butter, lemon-pepper and parsley flakes in small bowl. Pour over warm chicken; serve immediately with your favorite dipping sauce.

BANG-BANG CAULIFLOWER

MAKES 4 TO 6 SERVINGS

1 head cauliflower
½ cup mayonnaise
¼ cup sweet chili sauce
1½ teaspoons hot pepper sauce
¼ teaspoon salt

⅛ teaspoon black pepper
¼ cup all-purpose flour
1 cup panko bread crumbs
2 green onions, chopped

1 Trim greens and stems from cauliflower. Cut into florets.

2 Combine mayonnaise, chili sauce, hot pepper sauce, salt and black pepper in small bowl. Remove half of mixture; set aside. Place flour and panko in separate shallow dishes.

3 Preheat air fryer to 390°F. Line basket with parchment paper.

4 Lightly coat cauliflower in flour. Dip in sauce mixture, coat with panko.

5 Cook in batches 8 to 10 minutes or until cauliflower is softened and browned.

6 Place cauliflower on serving plate; sprinkle with green onions. Serve with reserved sauce mixture.

MACARONI AND CHEESE BITES

MAKES ABOUT 4 SERVINGS

4 ounces uncooked elbow macaroni

1 tablespoon butter

1 tablespoon all-purpose flour

1 cup milk

½ teaspoon salt, divided

1 cup (4 ounces) shredded Cheddar cheese

½ cup (2 ounces) shredded Swiss cheese

½ cup (2 ounces) shredded smoked Gouda cheese

2 eggs

2 tablespoons water

1 cup plain dry bread crumbs

½ teaspoon Italian seasoning

Marinara sauce, heated

1 Cook macaroni in large saucepan of boiling salted water 7 minutes or until al dente. Drain and set aside.

2 Melt butter in same saucepan over medium-high heat. Whisk in flour until smooth. Cook 1 minute, whisking frequently. Whisk in milk in thin, steady stream; cook over medium-high heat about 8 minutes or until thickened. Add ¼ teaspoon salt. Gradually stir in cheeses until melted and smooth. Stir in macaroni.

3 Spray 6×3-inch baking pan with nonstick cooking spray. Spread macaroni and cheese in prepared pan; smooth top. Cover with plastic wrap; refrigerate 4 hours or until firm and cold.

4 Turn out macaroni and cheese onto cutting board; cut into 1-inch pieces. Preheat air fryer to 370°F.

5 Whisk eggs and 2 tablespoons water in medium bowl. Combine bread crumbs, Italian seasoning and remaining ¼ teaspoon salt in shallow dish. Working with a few pieces at a time, dip macaroni and cheese pieces in egg mixture, then toss in bread crumb mixture to coat. Place on baking sheet.

6 Cook in batches 2 to 3 minutes or until golden brown. Serve warm with marinara sauce for dipping.

THE BIG ONION

MAKES 6 SERVINGS

DIPPING SAUCE

- ½ cup light mayonnaise
- 2 tablespoons horseradish
- 1 tablespoon ketchup
- ¼ teaspoon paprika
- ⅛ teaspoon salt
- ⅛ teaspoon ground red pepper
- ⅛ teaspoon dried oregano

ONION

- 1 large sweet onion (about 1 pound)
- ½ cup all-purpose flour
- 1 tablespoon buttermilk
- 2 eggs
- ½ cup panko bread crumbs
- 1 tablespoon paprika
- 1½ teaspoons seafood seasoning

1 For sauce, combine mayonnaise, horseradish, ketchup, ¼ teaspoon paprika, salt, ground red pepper and oregano in small bowl; mix well. Cover and refrigerate until ready to serve.

2 For onion, cut about ½ inch off top of onion and peel off papery skin. Place onion, cut side down, on cutting board. Starting ½ inch from root, use large sharp knife to make one slice almost down to cutting board. Repeat slicing all the way around onion to make 12 to 16 evenly spaced cuts. Turn onion over; gently separate outer pieces.

3 Meanwhile, put flour in large bowl. Whisk buttermilk and eggs in another large bowl. Combine panko, 1 tablespoon paprika and seafood seasoning in another bowl.

4 Coat onion with flour, shaking off any excess. Dip entire onion in egg mixture, letting excess drip back into bowl. Then coat evenly with panko mixture.

5 Preheat air fryer to 390°F. Spray basket with nonstick cooking spray.

6 Cook 10 to 12 minutes or until golden brown and crispy. Serve immediately with dipping sauce.

BUFFALO CAULIFLOWER BITES

MAKES 4 SERVINGS

½ cup all-purpose flour

½ cup water

½ teaspoon garlic powder

½ teaspoon salt

¼ teaspoon black pepper

1 small head cauliflower, cut into small florets

3 tablespoons hot pepper sauce

1 tablespoon melted butter

Chopped fresh parsley (optional)

Blue cheese dressing and celery sticks

1 Combine flour, water, garlic powder, salt and black pepper in large bowl; stir until mixed. Add cauliflower; stir until florets are well coated.

2 Preheat air fryer to 390°F. Line basket with parchment paper.

3 Cook 12 to 15 minutes, shaking occasionally during cooking, until florets are slightly tender and browned.

4 Meanwhile, combine hot pepper sauce and butter in medium bowl. Add warm florets; toss well.

5 Sprinkle with parsley, if desired. Serve with blue cheese dressing and celery sticks.

PEPPERONI STUFFED MUSHROOMS

MAKES 4 TO 6 SERVINGS

16 medium mushrooms

1 tablespoon olive oil

½ cup finely chopped onion

2 ounces pepperoni, finely chopped (about ½ cup)

¼ cup finely chopped green bell pepper

½ teaspoon seasoned salt

¼ teaspoon dried oregano

⅛ teaspoon black pepper

½ cup crushed buttery crackers (about 12)

¼ cup grated Parmesan cheese

1 tablespoon chopped fresh parsley, plus additional for garnish

1 Clean mushrooms; remove stems and set aside caps. Finely chop stems.

2 Heat oil in large skillet over medium-high heat. Add onion; cook and stir 2 to 3 minutes or until softened. Add mushroom stems, pepperoni, bell pepper, seasoned salt, oregano and black pepper; cook and stir 5 minutes or until vegetables are tender but not browned.

3 Remove from heat; stir in crushed crackers, Parmesan cheese and 1 tablespoon parsley until blended. Spoon mixture into mushroom caps, mounding slightly in centers.

4 Preheat air fryer to 370°F. Line basket with foil; spray with nonstick cooking spray.

5 Cook 6 to 8 minutes or until heated through. Garnish with additional parsley.

SHANGHAI CHICKEN WINGS
MAKES 4 TO 6 SERVINGS

SAUCE

- ½ cup water
- ½ tablespoon cornstarch
- 2 tablespoons packed dark brown sugar
- 2 tablespoons soy sauce
- 1½ tablespoons lime juice
- 1 tablespoon minced fresh ginger
- ½ teaspoon minced garlic
- ⅛ teaspoon red pepper flakes

CHICKEN

- 1 cup all-purpose flour
- ¼ cup cornstarch
- 2 teaspoons salt
- ¼ teaspoon black pepper
- ¼ teaspoon ground red pepper
- ¼ teaspoon paprika
- 2 eggs
- ½ cup milk
- 1 pound chicken drummettes or wings

1 For sauce, whisk water and ½ tablespoon cornstarch in medium saucepan until smooth. Add brown sugar, soy sauce, lime juice, ginger, garlic and red pepper flakes; whisk until well blended. Bring to a boil over high heat. Reduce heat to low; simmer 10 minutes or until thickened, stirring occasionally. Transfer to large bowl; set aside to cool.

2 For chicken, combine flour, ¼ cup cornstarch, salt, black pepper, ground red pepper and paprika in large bowl. Whisk eggs and milk in shallow bowl. Coat chicken with flour mixture. Dip in egg mixture, letting excess drip back into bowl. Coat again with flour mixture.

3 Preheat air fryer to 370°F. Spray chicken with nonstick cooking spray. Cook in batches 16 to 18 minutes, shaking halfway through cooking, until golden brown and cooked throughout. Brush sauce over warm chicken. Remove to serving plate.

MOZZARELLA STICKS

MAKES 12 SERVINGS

¼ cup all-purpose flour

2 eggs

1 tablespoon water

1 cup plain dry bread crumbs

2 teaspoons Italian seasoning

½ teaspoon salt

½ teaspoon garlic powder

1 package (12 ounces) string cheese (12 sticks)

1 cup marinara or pizza sauce, heated

1 Place flour in shallow dish. Whisk eggs and water in another shallow dish. Combine bread crumbs, Italian seasoning, salt and garlic powder in third shallow dish.

2 Coat each piece of cheese with flour. Dip in egg mixture, letting excess drip back into dish. Roll in bread crumb mixture to coat. Dip again in egg mixture and roll again in bread crumb mixture. Place on baking sheet. Refrigerate until ready to cook.

3 Preheat air fryer to 370°F. Line basket with parchment paper; spray with nonstick cooking spray.

4 Cook in batches 8 to 10 minutes, flipping halfway through cooking, until golden brown. Serve with marinara sauce.

AVOCADO EGG ROLLS

MAKES 10 SERVINGS AND 1 CUP SAUCE

DIPPING SAUCE

- ½ cup cashew nut pieces
- ½ cup packed fresh cilantro
- ¼ cup honey
- 2 green onions, coarsely chopped
- 2 cloves garlic
- 1 tablespoon white vinegar
- 1 teaspoon balsamic vinegar
- 1 teaspoon ground cumin
- ½ teaspoon tamarind paste
- ⅛ teaspoon ground turmeric
- ¼ cup olive oil

EGG ROLLS

- 2 avocados
- ¼ cup chopped drained oil-packed sun-dried tomatoes
- 2 tablespoons diced red onion
- 2 tablespoons chopped fresh cilantro
- 1 tablespoon lime juice
- ¼ teaspoon salt
- 10 wonton wrappers
  Vegetable oil

1 For sauce, combine cashews, ½ cup cilantro, honey, green onions, garlic, white vinegar, balsamic vinegar, cumin, tamarind paste and turmeric in food processor; process until coarsely chopped. With motor running, drizzle in olive oil in thin, steady stream; process until finely chopped and well blended. Refrigerate until ready to serve.

2 For egg rolls, place avocados in medium bowl; coarsely mash with potato masher. Stir in sun-dried tomatoes, red onion, 2 tablespoons chopped cilantro, lime juice and salt until well blended.

3 Working with one at a time, place wonton wrapper on work surface with one corner facing you. Spread 2 tablespoons filling horizontally across wrapper. Fold short sides over filling and fold up bottom corner over filling. Moisten top edges with water; roll up egg roll, pressing to seal. Refrigerate until ready to cook.

4 Preheat air fryer to 390°F. Brush egg rolls with vegetable oil.

5 Cook in batches 6 to 8 minutes, turning once, until golden brown and crispy. Cut egg rolls in half diagonally; serve with sauce.

PEPPERONI BREAD

MAKES ABOUT 6 SERVINGS

1 package (about 14 ounces) refrigerated pizza dough

8 slices provolone cheese

20 to 30 slices pepperoni (about ½ of 6-ounce package)

¾ cup (3 ounces) shredded mozzarella cheese

½ cup grated Parmesan cheese

½ teaspoon Italian seasoning

1 egg, beaten

Marinara sauce, heated

1 Unroll pizza dough on lightly floured surface; cut dough in half.

2 Working with one half at a time, arrange half the provolone slices on half the dough. Top with half the pepperoni, half the mozzarella and Parmesan cheese and half the Italian seasoning. Repeat with other half dough and toppings.

3 Fold top half of dough over filling; press edges with fork or pinch edges to seal.

4 Preheat air fryer to 390°F. Line basket with parchment paper. Transfer one bread to basket. Brush with egg.

5 Cook 8 to 10 minutes or until crust is golden brown. Remove to wire rack to cool slightly. Repeat with other bread. Cut crosswise into slices; serve warm with marinara sauce.

TOASTED RAVIOLI

1 cup all-purpose flour

2 eggs

¼ cup water

1 cup plain dry bread crumbs

1 teaspoon Italian seasoning

¾ teaspoon garlic powder

¼ teaspoon salt

½ cup grated Parmesan cheese

2 tablespoons finely chopped fresh parsley (optional)

1 package (10 ounces) cheese or meat ravioli, thawed if frozen

½ cup pasta sauce, heated

1 Place flour in shallow dish. Whisk eggs and water in another shallow dish. Combine bread crumbs, Italian seasoning, garlic powder and salt in third shallow dish. Combine Parmesan cheese and parsley, if desired, in large bowl.

2 Coat ravioli with flour. Dip in egg mixture, letting excess drip back into dish. Roll in bread crumb mixture to coat. Spray with nonstick cooking spray.

3 Preheat air fryer to 390°F. Poke holes in ravioli with toothpick.

4 Cook in batches 5 to 6 minutes, turning once, until golden brown. Add to bowl with cheese; toss to coat. Serve warm with sauce.

CINNAMON-SUGAR SWEET POTATO FRIES ▸

MAKES 2 TO 3 SERVINGS

1 sweet potato
1 teaspoon butter, melted
1 tablespoon cinnamon-sugar*

*To make cinnamon-sugar, combine 1 tablespoon sugar with ½ teaspoon ground cinnamon in small bowl.

1 Peel and cut the sweet potato into thin strips. Spray potato strips with nonstick cooking spray.

2 Preheat air fryer to 390°F. Cook potato strips 15 to 18 minutes in single layer, shaking occasionally, until potatoes are browned and crispy. Remove to medium bowl.

3 Toss potatoes with butter and cinnamon-sugar. Serve immediately.

INSPIRED BY BUCA® DI BEPPO ITALIAN RESTAURANT

CHEESY GARLIC BREAD

MAKES 4 TO 6 SERVINGS

1 loaf (about 8 ounces) Italian bread
¼ cup (½ stick) butter, softened
4 cloves garlic, diced

2 tablespoons grated Parmesan cheese
1 cup (4 ounces) shredded mozzarella cheese

1 Cut bread in half horizontally. Spread cut sides of bread evenly with butter; top with garlic. Sprinkle with Parmesan cheese and mozzarella.

2 Preheat air fryer to 370°F. Line basket with foil.

3 Cook 5 to 6 minutes or until cheese is melted and golden brown. Cut crosswise into slices. Serve warm.

BUFFALO WINGS
MAKES 4 SERVINGS

1 cup hot pepper sauce

⅓ cup vegetable oil, plus additional for brushing

1 teaspoon sugar

½ teaspoon ground red pepper

½ teaspoon garlic powder

½ teaspoon Worcestershire sauce

⅛ teaspoon black pepper

1 pound chicken wings, tips removed, split at joints

Blue cheese or ranch dressing

Celery sticks (optional)

1 Combine hot pepper sauce, ⅓ cup oil, sugar, red pepper, garlic powder, Worcestershire sauce and black pepper in small saucepan; cook over medium heat 20 minutes. Remove from heat; pour sauce into large bowl.

2 Preheat air fryer to 370°F. Brush wings with additional oil. Cook in batches 16 to 18 minutes or until golden brown and cooked throughout, shaking halfway through cooking.

3 Transfer wings to bowl of sauce; stir to coat. Serve with blue cheese dressing and celery sticks, if desired.

MEDITERRANEAN BAKED FETA
MAKES 4 TO 6 SERVINGS

Savory Pita Chips (recipe follows) or store-bought pita chips

1 package (8 ounces) feta cheese, cut crosswise into 4 slices

½ cup grape tomatoes, halved

¼ cup sliced roasted red peppers

¼ cup pitted kalamata olives

⅛ teaspoon dried oregano
   Black pepper

2 tablespoons extra virgin olive oil

1 tablespoon shredded fresh basil

1 Prepare Savory Pita Chips.

2 Preheat air fryer to 370°F.

3 Place cheese in small baking dish that fits inside air fryer; top with tomatoes, roasted peppers and olives. Sprinkle with oregano and season with black pepper; drizzle with oil.

4 Cook 6 to 8 minutes or until cheese is soft. Sprinkle with basil. Serve immediately with Savory Pita Chips.

SAVORY PITA CHIPS
MAKES 4 SERVINGS

2 whole wheat or white pita bread rounds

2 tablespoons grated Parmesan cheese (optional)

1 teaspoon dried basil

¼ teaspoon garlic powder

1 Carefully cut each pita round in half horizontally; split into two rounds. Cut each round into six wedges. Spray wedges with nonstick cooking spray.

2 Combine Parmesan cheese, if desired, basil and garlic powder in small bowl; sprinkle evenly over pita wedges.

3 Preheat air fryer to 350°F.

4 Cook 8 to 10 minutes, shaking occasionally during cooking, until golden brown. Cool completely.

CRAB RANGOON WITH SPICY DIPPING SAUCE

MAKES ABOUT 12 SERVINGS

DIPPING SAUCE

- 1 cup ketchup
- ¼ cup chili garlic sauce
- 4 teaspoons Chinese hot mustard

CRAB RANGOON

- 1 package (8 ounces) cream cheese, softened
- 1 can (6 ounces) lump crabmeat, well drained
- ⅓ cup minced green onions
- 1 package (12 ounces) wonton wrappers
- 1 egg white, beaten

1 Combine ketchup, chili garlic sauce and mustard in small bowl; mix well.

2 Beat cream cheese in medium bowl with electric mixer at medium speed until light and fluffy. Stir in crabmeat and green onions.

3 Arrange wonton wrappers, one at a time, on clean work surface. Place 1 rounded teaspoon crab mixture in center of wrapper. Brush inside edges of wonton wrapper with egg white. Fold wonton diagonally in half to form triangle* or crimp the corners up to meet in the center, forming a dumpling; press edges firmly to seal. Spray with nonstick cooking spray.

4 Preheat air fryer to 350°F. Spray basket with cooking spray. Cook in batches 6 to 8 minutes or until golden brown. Serve immediately with Dipping Sauce.

*Wonton wrappers are not quite square so they will not form perfect triangles.

CRAB SHACK DIP
MAKES 6 TO 8 SERVINGS (ABOUT 3½ CUPS)

Corn Tortilla Chips (recipe follows) or favorite tortilla chips

½ (8-ounce) package cream cheese, softened

½ cup sour cream

2 tablespoons mayonnaise

¾ teaspoon seasoned salt

¼ teaspoon paprika, plus additional for garnish

2 cans (6 ounces each) crabmeat, drained and flaked

½ cup (2 ounces) shredded mozzarella cheese

2 tablespoons minced onion

2 tablespoons finely chopped green bell pepper*

Chopped fresh parsley (optional)

For a spicier dip, substitute 1 tablespoon minced jalapeño pepper for the bell pepper.

1 Prepare Corn Tortilla Chips.

2 Combine cream cheese, sour cream, mayonnaise, seasoned salt and ¼ teaspoon paprika in medium bowl; stir until well blended and smooth. Add crabmeat, cheese, onion and bell pepper; stir until blended. Spread in small (1-quart) shallow baking dish.

3 Preheat air fryer to 330°F.

4 Cook 10 to 12 minutes or until bubbly and top is beginning to brown. Garnish with additional paprika and parsley; serve with Corn Tortilla Chips.

CORN TORTILLA CHIPS
MAKES 3 DOZEN CHIPS

6 (6-inch) corn tortillas, preferably day-old

½ teaspoon salt

1 If tortillas are fresh, let stand, uncovered, in single layer on wire rack 1 to 2 hours to dry slightly.

2 Stack tortillas; cut tortillas into six equal wedges. Spray tortillas generously with nonstick olive oil cooking spray.

3 Preheat air fryer to 370°F.

4 Cook in batches 5 to 6 minutes, shaking halfway through cooking. Sprinkle with salt.

MINI EGG ROLLS

MAKES 28 MINI EGG ROLLS

½ pound ground pork
3 cloves garlic, minced
1 teaspoon minced fresh ginger
¼ teaspoon red pepper flakes
6 cups (12 ounces) shredded coleslaw mix
¼ cup reduced-sodium soy sauce
1 tablespoon cornstarch
1 tablespoon seasoned rice vinegar
½ cup chopped green onions
28 wonton wrappers
Prepared sweet and sour sauce
Chinese hot mustard

1 Combine pork, garlic, ginger and red pepper flakes in large nonstick skillet; cook and stir over medium heat about 4 minutes or until pork is cooked through, stirring to break up meat. Add coleslaw mix; cover and cook 2 minutes. Uncover and cook 2 minutes or until coleslaw mix just begins to wilt.

2 Whisk soy sauce and cornstarch in small bowl until smooth and well blended; stir into pork mixture. Add vinegar; cook 2 to 3 minutes or until sauce is thickened. Remove from heat; stir in green onions.

3 Working with 1 wonton wrapper at a time, place wrapper on clean work surface. Spoon 1 tablespoon pork mixture across and just below center of wrapper. Fold bottom point of wrapper up over filling; fold side points over filling, forming envelope shape. Moisten inside edges of top point with water and roll egg roll toward top point, pressing firmly to seal. Repeat with remaining wrappers and filling. Spray egg rolls with nonstick cooking spray.

4 Preheat air fryer to 370°F. Cook in batches 3 to 5 minutes or until golden brown. Remove to cooling rack; cool slightly before serving. Serve with sweet and sour sauce and mustard for dipping.

BREAKFAST BITES

INSPIRED BY THE CHEESECAKE FACTORY®

RICOTTA PANCAKES

MAKES 8 TO 10 PANCAKES

1 package (15 ounces) whole milk
   ricotta cheese
1 egg
½ teaspoon vanilla
¼ cup granulated sugar

1 cup all-purpose flour, divided
¼ teaspoon baking powder
½ cup seedless raspberry jam
   Powdered sugar
   Fresh raspberries (optional)

1 Combine ricotta cheese and egg in large bowl; mix well. Add vanilla; stir. Add granulated sugar, ¾ cup flour and baking powder. Mix well. Put remaining ¼ cup flour in medium bowl.

2 Scoop about ¼ to ½ cup mixture into a ball. Add to bowl with flour; coat well. Flatten into pancake about ½ inch thick. Repeat with remaining batter. Spray with nonstick cooking spray.

3 Preheat air fryer to 370°F. Line basket with parchment paper.

4 Cook in batches 14 to 16 minutes until lightly browned, flipping and spraying with cooking spray after 10 minutes.

5 Place raspberry jam in small microwavable bowl; microwave on HIGH 30 seconds or until melted. Drizzle over warm pancakes. Sprinkle with powdered sugar. Garnish with raspberries, if desired.

HEARTY HASH BROWN CASSEROLE

MAKES ABOUT 16 SERVINGS

2 cups sour cream

2 cups (8 ounces) shredded Colby cheese, divided

1 can (10¾ ounces) cream of chicken soup

½ cup (1 stick) butter, melted

1 small onion, finely chopped

¾ teaspoon salt

½ teaspoon black pepper

1 package (30 ounces) frozen shredded hash brown potatoes, thawed

1 Preheat air fryer to 350°F. Spray 2 (1½-quart) baking dishes with nonstick cooking spray.

2 Combine sour cream, 1½ cups cheese, soup, butter, onion, salt and pepper in large bowl; mix well. Add potatoes; stir until well blended. Spread mixture in prepared baking dishes. (Do not pack down.) Sprinkle with remaining ½ cup cheese.

3 Cook in batches, if necessary, 30 to 35 minutes or until cheese is melted and top of casserole begin to brown.

BAKED APPLE PANCAKE

MAKES 2 TO 4 SERVINGS

3 tablespoons butter

3 medium Granny Smith apples (about 1¼ pounds), peeled and cut into ¼-inch slices

½ cup packed dark brown sugar

1½ teaspoons ground cinnamon

½ teaspoon plus pinch of salt, divided

4 eggs

⅓ cup whipping cream

⅓ cup milk

2 tablespoons granulated sugar

½ teaspoon vanilla

⅔ cup all-purpose flour

1 Melt butter in 8-inch nonstick skillet over medium heat. Add apples, brown sugar, cinnamon and pinch of salt; cook 8 minutes or until apples begin to soften, stirring occasionally. Cool 30 minutes. Spray 8-inch pie pan* with nonstick cooking spray. Spread apples in even layer in pie pan.

2 Whisk eggs in large bowl until foamy. Add cream, milk, granulated sugar, vanilla and remaining ½ teaspoon salt; whisk until blended. Sift flour into egg mixture; whisk until batter is well blended and smooth. Set aside 15 minutes.

3 Stir batter. Pour evenly over apple mixture. Preheat air fryer to 370°F.

4 Cook 8 to 10 minutes or until top is golden brown and pancake is loose around edge. Cool 1 minute; loosen edge of pancake with spatula, if necessary. Place large serving plate or cutting board on top of pie pan and invert pancake onto plate. Serve warm.

If your air fryer is on the smaller side, use 2 smaller baking dishes or ramekins.

CHEDDAR BISCUITS
MAKES 15 BISCUITS

2 cups all-purpose flour

1 tablespoon sugar

1 tablespoon baking powder

2¼ teaspoons garlic powder, divided

¾ teaspoon plus pinch of salt, divided

1 cup whole milk

½ cup (1 stick) plus 3 tablespoons butter, melted and divided

2 cups (8 ounces) shredded Cheddar cheese

½ teaspoon dried parsley flakes

1 Preheat air fryer to 370°F. Line basket with parchment paper.

2 Combine flour, sugar, baking powder, 2 teaspoons garlic powder and ¾ teaspoon salt in large bowl; mix well. Add milk and ½ cup melted butter; stir just until dry ingredients are moistened. Stir in cheese just until blended. Drop scant ¼ cupfuls of dough about 1½ inches apart onto prepared basket.

3 Cook in batches 6 to 8 minutes or until golden brown.

4 Meanwhile, combine remaining 3 tablespoons melted butter, ¼ teaspoon garlic powder, pinch of salt and parsley flakes in small bowl; brush over biscuits immediately after removing from oven. Serve warm.

QUICK JELLY-FILLED BISCUIT DOUGHNUT BALLS

MAKES 20 DOUGHNUT BALLS

1 package (about 7 ounces) refrigerated reduced-fat biscuit dough (10 biscuits)

¼ cup coarse sugar

1 cup strawberry preserves*

If preserves are very chunky, process in food processor 10 seconds or press through fine-mesh sieve.

1 Separate biscuits into 10 portions. Cut each in half; roll dough into balls to create 20 balls.

2 Preheat air fryer to 370°F.

3 Cook in batches 5 to 6 minutes or until golden brown.

4 Place sugar in large bowl. Coat warm balls in sugar. Let cool. Using a piping bag with medium star tip; fill bag with preserves. Poke hole in side of each doughnut ball with paring knife; fill with preserves. Serve immediately.

STRAWBERRY BANANA FRENCH TOAST

MAKES 2 SERVINGS

1 cup sliced fresh strawberries (about 8 medium)

2 teaspoons granulated sugar

2 eggs

½ cup milk

3 tablespoons all-purpose flour

1 teaspoon vanilla

⅛ teaspoon salt

4 slices (1 inch thick) egg bread or country bread

1 banana, cut into ¼-inch slices

Whipped cream and powdered sugar (optional)

Maple syrup

1 Combine strawberries and granulated sugar in small bowl; toss to coat. Set aside while preparing French toast.

2 Whisk eggs, milk, flour, vanilla and salt in shallow bowl or pie plate until well blended. Working with 2 slices at a time, dip bread into egg mixture, turning to coat completely; let excess drip off.

3 Preheat air fryer to 370°F. Cook 8 to 10 minutes or until golden brown. Repeat with remaining bread slices.

4 Top each serving with strawberry mixture and banana slices. Garnish with whipped cream and powdered sugar, if desired. Serve with maple syrup.

HEARTY SALADS

MEDITERRANEAN SALAD

MAKES 4 SERVINGS

2 boneless skinless chicken breasts
(about 4 ounces each)

Salt and black pepper (optional)

2 cups chopped iceberg lettuce

2 cups baby spinach

2 cups diced cucumbers

1 cup chopped roasted red peppers

1 cup grape tomatoes, halved

1 cup quartered artichoke hearts

¾ cup (3 ounces) crumbled feta cheese

½ cup chopped red onion

1 cup hummus

½ teaspoon Italian seasoning

1 Preheat air fryer to 370°F. Line basket with parchment paper.

2 Season chicken with salt and black pepper, if desired. Cook 12 to 15 minutes or until no longer pink in center and cooked throughout (165°F). Cool slightly; chop chicken.

3 Divide lettuce and spinach among 4 salad bowls or plates; top with cucumbers, chicken, roasted peppers, tomatoes, artichokes, cheese and onion.

4 Top salad with hummus; sprinkle with Italian seasoning.

ROASTED BRUSSELS SPROUTS SALAD

MAKES 6 SERVINGS

BRUSSELS SPROUTS

- 1 pound Brussels sprouts, trimmed and halved
- 2 tablespoons olive oil
- ½ teaspoon salt

SALAD

- 2 cups coarsely chopped baby kale
- 2 cups coarsely chopped romaine lettuce
- 1½ cups candied pecans*
- 1 cup halved red grapes
- 1 cup diced cucumbers
- ½ cup dried cranberries
- ½ cup fresh blueberries
- ½ cup chopped red onion
- ¼ cup toasted pumpkin seeds (pepitas)
- 1 container (4 ounces) crumbled goat cheese

DRESSING

- ½ cup olive oil
- 6 tablespoons balsamic vinegar
- 6 tablespoons strawberry jam
- 2 teaspoons Dijon mustard
- 1 teaspoon salt

Candied or glazed pecans may be found in the produce section of the supermarket with other salad toppings, or they may be found in the snack aisle.

1 For Brussels sprouts, preheat air fryer to 370°F. Spray basket with nonstick cooking spray.

2 Combine Brussels sprouts, 2 tablespoons oil and ½ teaspoon salt in medium bowl; toss to coat. Cook 15 to 18 minutes, shaking occasionally, or until tender and browned. Cool completely.

3 For salad, combine kale, lettuce, pecans, grapes, cucumbers, cranberries, blueberries, onion and pumpkin seeds in large bowl. Top with Brussels sprouts and cheese.

4 For dressing, whisk ½ cup oil, vinegar, jam, mustard and 1 teaspoon salt in small bowl until well blended. Pour dressing over salad; toss gently to coat.

AMADZING APPLE SALAD

MAKES 4 SERVINGS

DRESSING

- 5 tablespoons apple juice concentrate
- ¼ cup white balsamic vinegar
- 1 tablespoon lemon juice
- 1 tablespoon sugar
- 1 clove garlic, minced
- ½ teaspoon salt
- ½ teaspoon onion powder
- ¼ teaspoon ground ginger
- ¼ cup extra virgin olive oil

SALAD

- 4 boneless skinless chicken breasts (about 3 ounces each)
- Salt and black pepper (optional)
- 12 cups mixed greens such as chopped romaine lettuce and spring greens
- 2 tomatoes, cut into wedges
- 1 package (about 3 ounces) dried apple chips
- ½ red onion, thinly sliced
- ½ cup (2 ounces) crumbled gorgonzola or blue cheese
- ½ cup pecans, toasted

1 For dressing, whisk apple juice concentrate, vinegar, lemon juice, sugar, garlic, ½ teaspoon salt, onion powder and ginger in small bowl until blended. Slowly whisk in oil in thin, steady stream until well blended.

2 For salad, preheat air fryer to 370°F. Spray basket with nonstick cooking spray.

3 Season chicken with salt and pepper, if desired. Cook 12 to 15 minutes or until no longer pink in center and cooked throughout (165°F). Cool slightly; slice chicken.

4 Divide greens among 4 serving bowls. Top with chicken, tomatoes, apple chips, onion, cheese and pecans.

5 Drizzle about 2 tablespoons dressing over each salad.

SHRIMP AND SPINACH SALAD

MAKES 4 SERVINGS

3 to 4 slices bacon

DRESSING

¼ cup red wine vinegar

½ teaspoon cornstarch

¼ cup olive oil

¼ cup sugar

¼ teaspoon salt

¼ teaspoon black pepper

¼ teaspoon liquid smoke

SHRIMP

2 teaspoons black pepper

1 teaspoon salt

1 teaspoon garlic powder

½ teaspoon sugar

½ teaspoon onion powder

½ teaspoon ground sage

½ teaspoon paprika

20 to 24 large raw shrimp, peeled and deveined

2 tablespoons olive oil

SALAD

8 cups packed torn stemmed spinach

1 tomato, diced

½ red onion, thinly sliced

½ cup sliced roasted red peppers

1 Preheat air fryer to 400°F. Cook bacon 8 to 10 minutes or until crisp. Drain on paper towel-lined plate. Crumble bacon; set aside.

2 For dressing, stir vinegar into cornstarch in small bowl until smooth. Whisk in ¼ cup oil, ¼ cup sugar, ¼ teaspoon salt, ¼ teaspoon black pepper and liquid smoke until well blended.

3 For shrimp, combine 2 teaspoons black pepper, 1 teaspoon salt, garlic powder, ½ teaspoon sugar, onion powder, sage and paprika in medium bowl; mix well. Add shrimp; toss to coat.

4 Preheat air fryer to 390°F. Add shrimp; cook 6 to 8 minutes or until shrimp is pink and opaque.

5 For salad, combine spinach, tomato, onion and roasted peppers in large bowl. Add two thirds of dressing; toss to coat. Top with shrimp and crumbled bacon; serve with remaining dressing.

STRAWBERRY FIELDS SALAD

MAKES 4 SERVINGS

GLAZED WALNUTS

- 2 tablespoons butter, melted
- 6 tablespoons sugar
- 1 tablespoon honey
- ½ teaspoon salt
- ⅛ teaspoon ground red pepper
- 1 cup walnuts

DRESSING

- 1 cup fresh strawberries, hulled
- ½ cup vegetable oil
- 6 tablespoons white wine vinegar
- 3 tablespoons sugar
- 3 tablespoons honey
- 2 tablespoons balsamic vinegar
- 2 teaspoons Dijon mustard
- ½ teaspoon dried oregano
- ¼ teaspoon salt

SALAD

- 3 boneless skinless chicken breasts (about 4 ounces each)
  Salt and black pepper (optional)
- 4 cups chopped romaine lettuce
- 4 cups coarsely chopped fresh spinach
- 1 cup sliced fresh strawberries
- ½ cup (2 ounces) crumbled feta cheese

1 For walnuts, preheat air fryer to 325°F. Line basket with parchment paper.

2 Combine melted butter, 6 tablespoons sugar, 1 tablespoon honey, ½ teaspoon salt and red pepper in small bowl until well blended. Add walnuts; toss well. Cook 3 to 4 minutes or until nuts are glazed and begin to brown, shaking occasionally. Cool completely.

3 For dressing, combine whole strawberries, oil, white wine vinegar, 3 tablespoons sugar, 3 tablespoons honey, balsamic vinegar, mustard, oregano and ¼ teaspoon salt in blender or food processor; blend 30 seconds or until smooth.

4 Preheat air fryer to 370°F. Spray basket with nonstick cooking spray. Season chicken with salt and black pepper, if desired. Cook 12 to 15 minutes or until no longer pink in center and cooked throughout (165°F). Cool slightly; slice chicken.

5 For each salad, combine 1 cup lettuce and 1 cup spinach on serving plate; top with ¼ cup sliced strawberries, ¼ cup glazed walnuts and 2 tablespoons cheese. Drizzle with 2 tablespoons dressing; top with chicken.

BBQ CHICKEN SALAD

MAKES 4 SERVINGS

DRESSING

- ¾ cup light or regular mayonnaise
- ⅓ cup buttermilk
- ¼ cup sour cream
- 1 tablespoon white wine vinegar
- 1 teaspoon sugar
- ¼ teaspoon salt
- ¼ teaspoon garlic powder
- ¼ teaspoon onion powder
- ¼ teaspoon dried parsley flakes
- ¼ teaspoon dried dill weed
- ¼ teaspoon black pepper

SALAD

- 3 boneless skinless chicken breasts (about 4 ounces each)
- Salt and black pepper (optional)
- ½ cup barbecue sauce
- 4 cups chopped romaine lettuce
- 4 cups chopped iceberg lettuce
- 2 medium tomatoes, seeded and chopped
- ¾ cup canned or thawed frozen corn, drained
- ¾ cup diced jicama
- ¾ cup (3 ounces) shredded Monterey Jack cheese
- ¼ cup chopped fresh cilantro
- 2 green onions, sliced
- 1 cup crispy tortilla strips

1 For dressing, whisk mayonnaise, buttermilk, sour cream, vinegar, sugar, ¼ teaspoon salt, garlic powder, onion powder, parsley flakes, dill weed and ¼ teaspoon pepper in medium bowl until well blended. Cover and refrigerate until ready to serve.

2 Preheat air fryer to 370°F. Line basket with parchment paper. Season chicken with salt and pepper, if desired. Cook 12 to 15 minutes or until no longer pink in center and cooked throughout (165°F). Cool slightly; cut chicken into ½-inch pieces.

3 For salad, combine chicken and barbecue sauce in medium bowl; toss to coat.

4 Combine lettuce, tomatoes, corn, jicama, cheese and cilantro in large bowl. Add two thirds of dressing; toss to coat. Add remaining dressing, if necessary. Divide salad among 4 plates; top with chicken, green onions and tortilla strips.

SUPERFOOD KALE SALAD

MAKES 4 SERVINGS

MAPLE-ROASTED CARROTS

- 8 carrots, trimmed
- 2 tablespoons olive oil
- 2 tablespoons maple syrup
- ½ teaspoon salt
- ⅛ teaspoon black pepper
- Dash ground red pepper

CHICKEN

- 3 boneless skinless chicken breasts (about 4 ounces each)
- Salt and black pepper (optional)

MAPLE-LEMON VINAIGRETTE

- ¼ cup extra virgin olive oil
- 3 tablespoons lemon juice
- 2 tablespoons maple syrup
- ¾ teaspoon grated lemon peel
- ½ teaspoon salt
- ⅛ teaspoon black pepper

SALAD

- 4 cups chopped kale
- 2 cups chopped mixed greens
- 1 cup dried cranberries
- 1 cup slivered almonds, toasted*
- 1 cup shredded Parmesan cheese

To toast almonds, spread on ungreased baking sheet. Bake in preheated 350°F oven 6 to 8 minutes or until lightly browned, stirring occasionally.

1 Preheat oven to 370°F. Line basket with parchment paper.

2 Place carrots in shallow plate. Whisk 2 tablespoons oil, 2 tablespoons maple syrup, ½ teaspoon salt, ⅛ teaspoon black pepper and red pepper in small bowl until well blended. Brush some of oil mixture over carrots. Cook 18 to 20 minutes or until carrots are tender, occasionally shaking and brushing with oil mixture. Cut carrots crosswise into ¼-inch slices when cool enough to handle.

3 Season chicken with salt and black pepper, if desired. Cook 12 to 15 minutes or until no longer pink in center and cooked throughout (165°F). Cool slightly; slice chicken.

4 Prepare vinaigrette. Whisk ¼ cup oil, lemon juice, 2 tablespoons maple syrup, lemon peel, ½ teaspoon salt and ⅛ teaspoon black pepper in small bowl until well blended.

5 Combine kale, mixed greens, cranberries, almonds and cheese in large bowl. Add carrots. Pour vinaigrette over salad; toss to coat. Top with chicken.

CHICKEN WALDORF SALAD

MAKES 4 SERVINGS

DRESSING

- ⅓ cup balsamic vinegar
- 2 tablespoons Dijon mustard
- 2 teaspoons minced garlic
- ½ teaspoon salt
- ¼ teaspoon black pepper
- ⅔ cup extra virgin olive oil

SALAD

- 4 boneless skinless chicken breasts (about 4 ounces each)
- Salt and black pepper (optional)
- 8 cups mixed greens
- 1 large Granny Smith apple, cut into ½-inch pieces
- ⅔ cup diced celery
- ⅔ cup halved red seedless grapes
- ½ cup candied walnuts*
- ½ cup crumbled blue cheese

Candied or glazed walnuts maybe found in the produce section of the supermarket with other salad toppings, or they may be found in the snack aisle.

1 For dressing, combine vinegar, mustard, garlic, ½ teaspoon salt and ¼ teaspoon pepper in medium bowl; mix well. Slowly add oil, whisking until well blended.

2 Preheat air fryer to 370°F. Spray basket with nonstick cooking spray. Season chicken with salt and pepper, if desired. Cook 12 to 15 minutes or until no longer pink in center and cooked throughout (165°F). Cool slightly; slice chicken.

3 For salad, combine mixed greens, apple, celery and grapes in large bowl. Add half of dressing; toss to coat. Top with chicken, walnuts and cheese; drizzle with additional dressing.

AUTUMN HARVEST SALAD

MAKES 6 SERVINGS

DRESSING

- ½ cup extra virgin olive oil
- 3 tablespoons balsamic vinegar
- 1 clove garlic, minced
- 1 teaspoon honey
- 1 teaspoon Dijon mustard
- ½ teaspoon dried oregano
- ½ teaspoon salt
- ⅛ teaspoon black pepper

SALAD

- 1 loaf (12 to 16 ounces) artisan pecan raisin bread
- 4 tablespoons (½ stick) butter, melted
- 6 tablespoons coarse sugar (such as demerara, turbinado or organic cane sugar)
- 3 boneless skinless chicken breasts (about 4 ounces each)
  Salt and black pepper (optional)
- 6 cups packed spring greens
- 2 Granny Smith apples, thinly sliced
- ¾ cup crumbled blue cheese
- ¾ cup dried cranberries
- ¾ cup toasted walnuts*

To toast nuts, cook in preheated 325°F parchment-lined air fryer 3 to 4 minutes or until golden brown.

1 For dressing, whisk oil, vinegar, garlic, honey, mustard, oregano, ½ teaspoon salt and ⅛ teaspoon pepper in medium bowl until well blended. Refrigerate until ready to use.

2 Preheat air fryer to 330°F. Line basket with parchment paper. Cut bread into thin (¼-inch) slices. Brush each slice with melted butter and sprinkle with 1 teaspoon sugar. Place in single layer in prepared basket. Cook in batches 6 to 8 minutes or until crisp. Cool completely.

3 Preheat air fryer to 370°F. Season chicken with salt and pepper, if desired. Cook 12 to 15 minutes or until no longer pink in center and cooked throughout (165°F). Cut chicken into thin strips.

4 For each salad, place 1 cup greens on serving plate. Top with ½ cup apple slices, ¼ cup chicken strips and 2 tablespoons each cheese, cranberries and walnuts. Break 2 toast slices into pieces and sprinkle over salad. Drizzle with 2 tablespoons dressing.

STRAWBERRY POPPY SEED CHICKEN SALAD

MAKES 4 SERVINGS

DRESSING

- ¼ cup white wine vinegar
- 2 tablespoons orange juice
- 1 tablespoon sugar
- 2 teaspoons poppy seeds
- 1½ teaspoons Dijon mustard
- ½ teaspoon salt
- ½ teaspoon minced dried onion
- ½ cup vegetable oil

SALAD

- 4 boneless skinless chicken breasts (about 4 ounces each)
- Salt and black pepper (optional)
- 8 cups romaine lettuce
- ¾ cup fresh pineapple chunks
- ¾ cup sliced fresh strawberries
- ¾ cup fresh blueberries
- 1 navel orange, peeled and sectioned *or* 1 can (11 ounces) mandarin oranges, drained
- ¼ cup chopped toasted pecans*

*To toast nuts, cook in preheated 325°F parchment-lined air fryer 3 to 4 minutes or until golden brown.

1 For dressing, combine vinegar, orange juice, sugar, poppy seeds, mustard, ½ teaspoon salt and dried onion in small bowl; mix well. Whisk in oil in thin, steady stream until well blended.

2 Preheat air fryer to 370°F. Spray basket with nonstick cooking spray. Season chicken with salt and pepper, if desired. Cook 12 to 15 minutes or until no longer pink and cooked throughout (165°F). Cool slightly; slice chicken.

3 For salad, combine lettuce and two thirds of dressing in large bowl; toss gently to coat. Divide salad among 4 plates, top with chicken, pineapple, strawberries, blueberries, oranges and pecans. Serve with remaining dressing.

SANDWICHES & SMALL BITES

INSPIRED BY TGI FRIDAYS™

TUSCAN PORTOBELLO MELT

MAKES 2 SERVINGS

- 1 portobello mushroom cap, thinly sliced
- ½ small red onion, thinly sliced
- ½ cup grape tomatoes
- 1 tablespoon olive oil
- 1 teaspoon balsamic vinegar
- ⅛ teaspoon salt
- ⅛ teaspoon dried thyme
- ⅛ teaspoon black pepper
- 2 tablespoons butter, softened and divided
- 4 slices sourdough bread
- 2 slices provolone cheese
- 2 teaspoons Dijon mustard
- 2 slices Monterey Jack cheese

1 Combine mushroom, onion and tomatoes in small bowl. Drizzle with oil and vinegar; sprinkle with salt, thyme and pepper. Toss to coat.

2 Preheat air fryer to 390°F. Spray basket with nonstick cooking spray. Cook vegetables 8 to 10 minutes or until tender.

3 Brush butter on bread slices. Cook bread 2 to 4 minutes or until bread is golden brown. Transfer bread to cutting board.

4 Place provolone cheese on 2 bread slices; spread mustard over cheese. Top with vegetables, Monterey Jack cheese and remaining bread slices. Cook sandwiches 1 to 2 minutes or until cheese is melted.

NASHVILLE-STYLE HOT CHICKEN SANDWICH

MAKES 4 TO 6 SERVINGS

2 tablespoons hot pepper sauce, divided

2 tablespoons dill pickle juice, divided

1 teaspoon salt, divided

2 pounds chicken breast strips or tenders

1 cup all-purpose flour

½ teaspoon black pepper

1 egg

½ cup buttermilk

¼ cup olive oil

1 tablespoon red pepper flakes

1 tablespoon packed brown sugar

½ teaspoon paprika

½ teaspoon chili powder

¼ teaspoon garlic powder

4 to 6 Brioche buns, toasted

White Cheddar cheese slices (optional)

Sweet coleslaw and dill pickle slices

1 Combine 1 tablespoon hot pepper sauce, 1 tablespoon pickle juice and ½ teaspoon salt in large resealable food storage bag. Add chicken; seal and turn to coat. Refrigerate 1 hour to overnight.

2 Combine flour, remaining ½ teaspoon salt and black pepper in shallow dish. Whisk egg, buttermilk, remaining 1 tablespoon hot pepper sauce and remaining 1 tablespoon pickle juice in another shallow dish. Remove chicken from marinade; discard marinade. Coat chicken with flour mixture, then dip in egg mixture and again in flour mixture.

3 Preheat air fryer to 390°F. Spray basket with nonstick cooking spray. Cook chicken in batches 18 to 20 minutes or until no longer pink in center and cooked throughout (165°F), turning chicken halfway through cooking and spraying occasionally with cooking spray. Remove chicken to large platter.

4 Combine oil, red pepper flakes, brown sugar, paprika, chili powder and garlic powder in small bowl; pour over chicken.

5 Serve chicken on toasted bun with cheese, if desired, coleslaw and pickles.

CHICKEN FAJITA ROLL-UPS

MAKES 4 SERVINGS

1 cup ranch dressing

1 teaspoon chili powder

1 tablespoon vegetable oil

2 teaspoons lime juice

2 teaspoons fajita seasoning mix

½ teaspoon chipotle chili powder

¼ teaspoon salt

4 boneless skinless chicken breasts (about 6 ounces each)

4 fajita-size flour tortillas (8 to 9 inches), warmed

1 cup (4 ounces) shredded Cheddar cheese

1 cup (4 ounces) shredded Monterey Jack cheese

3 cups shredded lettuce

1 cup pico de gallo

1 Combine ranch dressing and chili powder in small bowl; mix well. Refrigerate until ready to serve.

2 Combine oil, lime juice, fajita seasoning mix, chipotle chili powder and salt in small bowl; mix well. Coat both sides of chicken with spice mixture.

3 Preheat air fryer to 370°F. Cook chicken 12 to 15 minutes or until no longer pink in center and cooked throughout (165°F). Remove to plate; let stand 5 minutes before slicing. Cut chicken breasts in half lengthwise, then cut crosswise into ½-inch strips.

4 Sprinkle each tortilla with ¼ cup Cheddar and ¼ cup Monterey Jack. Cook in batches 1 to 2 minutes or until cheese is melted. Remove tortilla to clean work surface or cutting board.

5 Sprinkle ¾ cup shredded lettuce down center of each tortilla; top each with ¼ cup pico de gallo and equal amounts of chicken. Fold bottom of tortilla up over filling, then fold in sides and roll up. Cut in half diagonally. Serve with ranch dipping sauce.

MUSHROOM PO-BOYS
MAKES 4 SERVINGS

Remoulade Sauce (recipe follows)*
1 cup buttermilk
1 tablespoon hot pepper sauce
1¼ cups all-purpose flour
1 teaspoon salt
1 teaspoon smoked paprika
¼ teaspoon onion powder
¼ teaspoon black pepper
1 package (4 ounces) sliced shiitake mushrooms

1 package (3 ounces) oyster mushrooms, cut into 2-inch or bite-size pieces
1 loaf French bread, ends trimmed, cut into 4 pieces and split
Sliced fresh tomatoes and finely shredded iceberg lettuce

*Or substitute plain mayonnaise for serving.

1 Prepare Remoulade Sauce; cover and refrigerate until ready to use.

2 Combine buttermilk and 1 tablespoon hot pepper sauce in medium bowl. Whisk flour, salt, paprika, onion powder and black pepper in another medium bowl. Dip mushroom pieces, a few at a time, in buttermilk mixture; roll in flour mixture to coat. Dip again in buttermilk mixture and roll in flour mixture; place on plate. Repeat until all mushrooms are coated.

3 Preheat air fryer to 370°F. Line basket with parchment paper; spray with nonstick cooking spray. Working in batches if necessary, arrange mushrooms in single layer in basket; spray tops with nonstick cooking spray. Cook 8 to 10 minutes or until coating is crisp and browned.

4 Serve mushrooms on French bread with tomatoes, lettuce and Remoulade sauce.

REMOULADE SAUCE
Combine ½ cup mayonnaise, 2 tablespoons Dijon or coarse grain mustard, 1 tablespoon lemon juice, 1 clove garlic, minced, and ½ teaspoon hot pepper sauce in small bowl.

SPINACH FLORENTINE FLATBREAD

MAKES 8 SERVINGS

1 tablespoon olive oil

2 cloves garlic, minced

1 package (10 ounces) baby spinach

1 can (about 14 ounces) quartered artichoke hearts, drained and sliced

½ teaspoon salt

¼ teaspoon dried oregano

Pinch black pepper

Pinch red pepper flakes

2 rectangular pizza or flatbread crusts (about 8 ounces each)

1 plum tomato, seeded and diced

2 cups (8 ounces) shredded Monterey Jack cheese

½ cup (2 ounces) shredded Italian cheese blend

Shredded fresh basil leaves (optional)

1 Heat oil in large skillet over medium-high heat. Add garlic; cook and stir 30 seconds. Add half of spinach; cook and stir until slightly wilted. Add additional spinach by handfuls; cook 3 minutes or until completely wilted, stirring occasionally. Remove to medium bowl; stir in artichokes, salt and oregano. Season with black pepper and red pepper flakes.

2 Preheat air fryer to 370°F. Line basket with parchment paper.

3 Place pizza crusts* in basket. Spread spinach mixture over crusts; sprinkle with tomato, Monterey Jack cheese and Italian cheese blend.

4 Cook 6 to 8 minutes or until cheese is melted and edges of crusts are browned. Garnish with basil.

*If your air fryer is on the smaller side, you may need to cut the crusts in half.

SEASONED CHICKEN SANDWICH
MAKES 4 SERVINGS

2 boneless skinless chicken breasts (4 to 6 ounces each)

4 cups cold water

¼ cup granulated sugar

3 tablespoons plus 1 teaspoon salt, divided

1 cup milk

2 eggs

1½ cups all-purpose flour

2 tablespoons powdered sugar

2 teaspoons paprika

2 teaspoons black pepper

¾ teaspoon baking powder

½ teaspoon ground red pepper

8 dill pickle slices

4 soft hamburger buns, toasted and buttered

1 Pound chicken to ½-inch thickness between 2 sheets of waxed paper or plastic wrap with rolling pin or meat mallet. Cut each breast in half crosswise to create total of 4 pieces.

2 Combine water, granulated sugar and 3 tablespoons salt in medium bowl; stir until sugar and salt are dissolved. Add chicken to brine; cover and refrigerate 2 to 4 hours. Remove chicken from refrigerator about 30 minutes before cooking.

3 Beat milk and eggs in medium shallow dish until blended. Combine flour, powdered sugar, paprika, black pepper, remaining 1 teaspoon salt, baking powder and red pepper in another shallow dish; mix well.

4 Working with one piece at a time, remove chicken from brine and add to milk mixture, turning to coat. Place in flour mixture; turn to coat completely and shake off excess.

5 Preheat air fryer to 370°F. Line basket with parchment paper. Place chicken in prepared basket, spraying with nonstick cooking spray. Cook 12 to 15 minutes, flipping halfway through cooking, until golden brown and crispy and cooked throughout (165°F).

6 Place 2 pickle slices on bottom halves of buns; top with chicken and top halves of buns. Serve immediately.

CUBAN PORK SANDWICH

MAKES 4 SERVINGS

⅓ cup orange juice

3 tablespoons lime juice

1 small onion, finely chopped (½ cup)

3 tablespoons olive oil

6 cloves garlic, minced

2 teaspoons ground cumin

2 teaspoons dried oregano

1 teaspoon salt

1 teaspoon black pepper

2 pounds boneless pork shoulder

4 Cuban sandwich rolls, split*

⅓ cup mayonnaise

⅓ cup yellow mustard

8 ounces sliced Swiss cheese

8 ounces sliced honey ham

8 long thin dill pickle slices

If Cuban rolls are unavailable, substitute a long French or Italian loaf, split in half horizontally and cut into 4 pieces.

1 Combine orange juice, lime juice, onion, oil, garlic, cumin, oregano, salt and pepper in medium bowl; mix well. Place pork in large resealable food storage bag. Pour marinade over pork; seal bag and turn to coat. Marinate in refrigerator at least 2 hours or overnight.

2 Preheat air fryer to 350°F. Line basket with heavy-duty foil. Place pork in basket; cook 40 to 50 minutes or until pork is tender and temperature reaches 160°F. Let stand at least 15 minutes before slicing. (Pork can be prepared in advance and refrigerated.)

3 Slice pork. (About half of pork is needed for sandwiches; reserve remaining pork for another use.) Spread both cut sides of rolls with mayonnaise, then mustard. Top bottom halves of rolls with half of cheese, ham, pickles, pork, remaining cheese and top halves of rolls.

4 Return sandwiches to air fryer. Cook 3 to 5 minutes or until bread is browned and crisp.

CHICKEN AND AVOCADO OVERSTUFFED QUESADILLAS

MAKES 2 SERVINGS

1 boneless skinless chicken breast (about 3 ounces)

Salt and black pepper (optional)

3 tablespoons Caesar dressing

2 teaspoons finely chopped fresh cilantro

2 burrito-size flour tortillas (10 to 11 inches)

¾ cup (3 ounces) shredded Monterey Jack cheese, divided

½ cup shredded green cabbage

½ cup pico de gallo

1 avocado, sliced

1 Preheat air fryer to 370°F. Spray basket with nonstick cooking spray.

2 Season chicken with salt and pepper, if desired. Cook 12 to 15 minutes or until no longer pink in center and cooked throughout (165°F). Cool slightly. Slice chicken; set aside.

3 Combine dressing and cilantro in small bowl; mix well. Roll up tortillas in paper towel or waxed paper; microwave on HIGH 10 seconds or until softened.

4 Place tortillas on work surface. For each quesadilla, sprinkle ¼ cup cheese in circle in center of tortilla, leaving 3-inch border all around. Top with half of chicken; drizzle with half of dressing mixture. Top with half each of cabbage, pico de gallo and avocado; sprinkle with 2 tablespoons cheese.

5 Working with one tortilla at a time, fold top of tortilla down over filling to center. Hold folded part down while working in clockwise direction, folding next section of tortilla in towards center until filling is completely covered. (You should end up with five folds and a hexagonal shape. If there is an uncovered hole in center of tortilla after folding, cut round piece from another tortilla to cover it.)

6 Preheat air fryer to 370°F. Spray quesadilla with cooking spray. Cook quesadilla, folded side down, 2 to 3 minutes or until golden brown, pressing down with spatula halfway through cooking. Flip and cook 2 to 3 minutes or until top is golden brown. Repeat with remaining quesadilla.

HEARTY VEGGIE SANDWICH

MAKES 4 SERVINGS

1 pound cremini mushrooms, stemmed and thinly sliced (⅛-inch slices)

2 teapoons olive oil, divided

¾ teaspoon salt, divided

¼ teaspoon black pepper

1 medium zucchini, diced (¼-inch pieces, about 2 cups)

3 tablespoons butter, softened

8 slices artisan whole grain bread

¼ cup pesto

¼ cup mayonnaise

2 cups packed baby spinach

4 slices (1 ounce each) mozzarella cheese

1 Preheat air fryer to 370°F. Combine mushrooms, 1 teaspoon oil, ½ teaspoon salt and pepper in medium bowl; toss to coat. Cook 6 to 8 minutes or until mushrooms are dark brown and dry, shaking occasionally. Remove to medium bowl.

2 Toss remaining 1 teaspoon oil, zucchini and remaining ¼ teaspoon salt in small bowl . Cook 2 to 4 minutes or until zucchini is tender and lightly browned. Remove to bowl.

3 Spread butter on one side of each bread slice. Turn over slices. Spread pesto on 4 bread slices; spread mayonnaise on remaining 4 slices. Top pesto-covered slices evenly with mushrooms; layer with spinach, zucchini and cheese. Top with remaining bread slices, mayonnaise side down.

4 Cook 2 to 4 minutes or until bread is toasted, spinach is slightly wilted and cheese is beginning to melt. Serve immediately.

NEW ORLEANS-STYLE MUFFALETTA

MAKES 4 TO 6 SERVINGS

¾ cup pitted green olives

½ cup pitted kalamata olives

½ cup giardiniera (Italian-style pickled vegetables), drained

2 tablespoons fresh parsley leaves

2 tablespoons capers

1 clove garlic, minced

2 tablespoons olive oil

1 tablespoon red wine vinegar

1 (8-inch) round Italian loaf (16 to 22 ounces)

8 ounces thinly sliced ham

8 ounces thinly sliced Genoa salami

6 ounces thinly sliced provolone cheese

1 Combine olives, giardiniera, parsley, capers and garlic in food processor; pulse until coarsely chopped and no large pieces remain. Transfer to small bowl; stir in oil and vinegar until well blended. Cover and refrigerate several hours or overnight to blend flavors.

2 Cut bread in half crosswise. Spread two thirds of olive salad over bottom half of bread; layer with ham, salami and cheese. Spread remaining olive salad over cheese; top with top half of bread, pressing down slightly to compress. Wrap sandwich with plastic wrap; let stand 1 hour to blend flavors.

3 To serve sandwich warm, preheat air fryer to 330°F. Remove plastic wrap; wrap sandwich loosely in foil. Cook 3 to 5 minutes or just until sandwich is slightly warm and cheese begins to melt. Cut into wedges.

CHICKEN PESTO FLATBREADS

MAKES 2 SERVINGS

2 boneless skinless chicken breasts (3 to 4 ounces each)

Salt and black pepper (optional)

2 (6- to 7-inch) round flatbreads or Greek-style pita bread rounds (no pocket)

2 tablespoons prepared pesto

4 slices (1 ounce each) mozzarella cheese

1 plum tomato, cut into ¼-inch slices

3 tablespoons shredded Parmesan cheese

1 Preheat air fryer to 370°F. Spray basket with nonstick cooking spray.

2 Season chicken with salt and pepper, if desired. Cook 12 to 15 minutes or until no longer pink in center and cooked throughout (165°F). Cool slightly; slice chicken.

3 Place flatbreads on work surface. Spread 1 tablespoon pesto over half of each flatbread. Place chicken on opposite half of bread; top with mozzarella, tomato and Parmesan cheese. Fold pesto-topped bread half over filling.

4 Preheat air fryer to 370°F. Spray flatbread with cooking spray. Cook sandwiches 2 to 3 minutes per side or until flatbread is browned, cheese begins to melt and sandwiches are heated through.

CHICKEN PARMESAN SLIDERS

MAKES 12 SLIDERS

4 boneless skinless chicken breasts (4 to 6 ounces each)

¼ cup all-purpose flour

2 eggs

1 tablespoon water

1 cup Italian-seasoned dry bread crumbs

½ cup grated Parmesan cheese

Salt and black pepper

Olive oil

12 slider buns (about 3 inches), split

¾ cup marinara sauce

6 tablespoons Alfredo sauce

6 slices (1 ounce each) mozzarella cheese, cut into halves

6 tablespoons pesto

2 tablespoons butter, melted

¼ teaspoon garlic powder

1 Pound chicken to ½-inch thickness between 2 sheets of waxed paper or plastic wrap with rolling pin or meat mallet. Cut each chicken breast crosswise into 3 pieces about the size of slider buns.

2 Place flour in shallow dish. Beat eggs and water in second shallow dish. Combine bread crumbs and Parmesan cheese in third shallow dish. Season flour and egg mixtures with pinch of salt and pepper. Coat chicken pieces lightly with flour, shaking off excess. Dip in egg mixture, coating completely; roll in bread crumb mixture to coat. Place on large plate; let stand 10 minutes.

3 Preheat air fryer to 370°F. Line basket with foil.

4 Cook chicken in batches, if necessary, 10 to 12 minutes, flipping halfway through cooking until golden brown and cooked throughout (165°F). Remove chicken.

5 Arrange slider buns on foil-lined basket with bottoms cut sides up and tops cut sides down. Spread 1 tablespoon marinara sauce over each bottom bun; top with piece of chicken. Spread ½ tablespoon Alfredo sauce over chicken; top with half slice of mozzarella. Spread ½ tablespoon pesto over cheese; cover with top buns.

6 Combine butter and garlic powder in small bowl; brush mixture over top buns. Cook 1 to 2 minutes or until cheese is melted and top buns are lightly browned.

BLT SUPREME
MAKES 2 SERVINGS

12 to 16 slices thick-cut bacon
⅓ cup mayonnaise
1½ teaspoons minced chipotle pepper in adobo sauce
1 teaspoon lime juice
1 ripe avocado
⅛ teaspoon salt

⅛ teaspoon black pepper
4 leaves romaine lettuce
½ baguette, cut into 2 (8-inch) lengths *or* 2 hoagie rolls, split and toasted
6 to 8 slices tomato

1 Preheat air fryer to 390°F. Cook bacon in batches 8 to 10 minutes or until crisp-chewy. Drain on paper towel-lined plate.

2 Meanwhile, combine mayonnaise, chipotle pepper and lime juice in small bowl; mix well. Coarsely mash avocado in another small bowl; stir in salt and black pepper. Cut romaine leaves crosswise into ¼-inch strips.

3 For each sandwich, spread heaping tablespoon mayonnaise mixture on bottom half of baguette; top with one fourth of lettuce. Arrange 3 to 4 slices bacon over lettuce; spread 2 tablespoons mashed avocado over bacon. Drizzle with heaping tablespoon mayonnaise mixture. Top with 3 to 4 tomato slices, one fourth of lettuce and 3 to 4 slices bacon. Close sandwich with top half of baguette.

ALMOND CHICKEN SALAD SANDWICH

MAKES 4 SERVINGS

¼ cup mayonnaise

¼ cup plain Greek yogurt or sour cream

2 tablespoons cider vinegar

1 tablespoon honey

1 teaspoon salt

½ teaspoon black pepper

⅛ teaspoon garlic powder

2 skinless boneless chicken breasts (about 4 ounces each)

Salt and black pepper (optional)

¾ cup halved red grapes

1 large stalk celery, chopped

⅓ cup sliced almonds

Leaf lettuce

1 tomato, thinly sliced

8 slices sesame semolina or country Italian bread

1 Whisk mayonnaise, yogurt, vinegar, honey, 1 teaspoon salt, ½ teaspoon pepper and garlic powder in small bowl until well blended.

2 Preheat air fryer to 370°F. Spray basket with nonstick cooking spray.

3 Season chicken with salt and pepper, if desired. Cook 12 to 15 minutes or until no longer pink in center and cooked throughout (165°F). Cool slightly; cut into small chunks.

4 Combine chicken, grapes and celery in medium bowl. Add dressing; toss gently to coat. Cover and refrigerate several hours or overnight. Stir in almonds just before making sandwiches.

5 Place lettuce and tomato slices on 4 bread slices; top with chicken salad and remaining bread slices. Serve immediately.

CLASSIC PATTY MELTS
MAKES 4 SERVINGS

4 tablespoons (½ stick) butter, divided and melted

2 large yellow onions, thinly sliced

¾ teaspoon plus pinch of salt, divided

1 pound ground chuck (80% lean)

½ teaspoon garlic powder

½ teaspoon onion powder

¼ teaspoon black pepper

8 slices marble rye bread

½ cup Thousand Island dressing

8 slices (1 ounce each) deli American or Swiss cheese

1 Preheat air fryer to 370°F.

2 Combine 2 tablespoons melted butter, onions and pinch of salt in large bowl; cook 12 to 15 minutes, shaking and tossing occasionally, until onions are very soft and golden brown. Remove to bowl.

3 Combine beef, remaining ¾ teaspoon salt, garlic powder, onion powder and pepper in medium bowl; mix gently. Shape into 4 (¼- to ½-inch thick) patties.

4 Cook patties 12 to 14 minutes, flipping halfway through cooking, until browned and cooked throughout (160°F).

5 Brush remaining 2 tablespoons melted butter on outside of each bread slice. Spread dressing on inside of bread slices. Layer 4 bread slices with cheese slice, patty, caramelized onions, another cheese slice and remaining bread slices.

6 Cook 2 to 4 minutes or until bread is golden brown and cheese is melted, flipping halfway through cooking.

CHICKEN BACON QUESADILLAS

4 teaspoons vegetable oil, divided

4 (8-inch) flour tortillas

1 cup (4 ounces) shredded Colby-Jack cheese

1 cup coarsely chopped cooked chicken

4 slices bacon, crisp-cooked and coarsely chopped*

½ cup pico de gallo, plus additional for serving

Sour cream and guacamole (optional)

Cook bacon in preheated 390°F air fryer 6 to 8 minutes or until crispy. Remove to paper towel-lined plate. Cool completely.

1 Preheat air fryer to 370°F. Spray basket with nonstick cooking spray.

2 Brush oil over each side of tortillas. Sprinkle one tortilla with ¼ cup cheese. Top with ¼ cup chicken, one fourth of bacon and 2 tablespoons pico de gallo. Fold tortilla in half.

3 Cook in batches 3 to 4 minutes or until cheese is melted and tortilla is lightly browned. Remove to cutting board; cool slightly. Cut into wedges. Repeat with remaining ingredients. Serve with additional pico de gallo, sour cream and guacamole, if desired.

CHICKEN AND ROASTED TOMATO PANINI

MAKES 4 SERVINGS

12 ounces plum tomatoes (about 2 large), cut into ⅛-inch slices

½ teaspoon coarse salt, divided

¼ teaspoon black pepper, divided

1 tablespoon olive oil, divided

4 boneless skinless chicken breasts (about 4 ounces each)

3 tablespoons butter, softened

¼ teaspoon garlic powder

¼ cup mayonnaise

2 tablespoons pesto

8 slices sourdough or rustic Italian bread

8 slices (about 1 ounce each) provolone cheese

½ cup baby spinach

1 Preheat air fryer to 350°F. Line basket with parchment paper. Sprinkle tomatoes with ¼ teaspoon salt and ⅛ teaspoon pepper; drizzle with oil. Cook in batches 8 to 10 minutes or until tomatoes are softened and begin to caramelize around edges.

2 Meanwhile, prepare chicken. If chicken breasts are thicker than ½ inch, pound to ½-inch thickness between 2 sheets of waxed paper or plastic wrap with rolling pin or meat mallet. Increase temperature on air fryer to 370°F. Season both sides of chicken with remaining ¼ teaspoon salt and ⅛ teaspoon pepper. Cook 12 to 15 minutes or until no longer pink in center and cooked throughout (165°F). Remove to plate; let stand 10 minutes before slicing. Cut diagonally into ½-inch slices.

3 Combine butter and garlic powder in small bowl; mix well. Combine mayonnaise and pesto in another small bowl; mix well.

4 Spread one side of each bread slice with garlic butter. For each sandwich, place 1 bread slice, buttered side down, on plate. Spread with generous 1 tablespoon pesto mayonnaise. Layer with 1 cheese slice, 4 to 5 roasted tomato slices, 4 to 6 spinach leaves, 1 sliced chicken breast, second cheese slice and 4 to 6 spinach leaves. Top with second bread slice, buttered side up.

5 Cook sandwiches 2 to 4 minutes or until bread is golden brown and cheese is melted.

GUACAMOLE BURGERS

MAKES 4 SERVINGS

1 small avocado

2 tablespoons finely chopped tomato

1 tablespoon chopped fresh cilantro

2 teaspoons lime juice, divided

1 teaspoon minced jalapeño pepper

¼ teaspoon salt, divided

2 tablespoons sour cream

2 tablespoons mayonnaise

½ teaspoon ground cumin

1 medium onion, cut into thin slices

1 small green bell pepper, cut into thin slices

1 small red bell pepper, cut into thin slices

2 teaspoons vegetable oil

1¼ pounds ground beef

Salt and black pepper

4 slices Monterey Jack cheese

4 hamburger buns, split and toasted

1 can (4 ounces) diced fire-roasted jalapeño peppers, drained

1 Mash avocado in medium bowl. Stir in tomato, cilantro, 1 teaspoon lime juice, minced jalapeño and ⅛ teaspoon salt; mix well. Cover; refrigerate until ready to use. Combine sour cream, mayonnaise, remaining 1 teaspoon lime juice and cumin in small bowl; mix well. Cover; refrigerate until ready to use.

2 Preheat air fryer to 390°F. Toss onion and bell peppers with oil in medium bowl. Cook 10 to 12 minutes or until vegetables are tender and begin to turn golden brown, shaking occasionally. Remove to bowl. Season vegetables with remaining ⅛ teaspoon salt.

3 Preheat air fryer to 370°F. Shape beef into 4 (5-inch) patties; sprinkle both sides generously with salt and black pepper. Cook patties 12 to 14 minutes or until cooked throughout (160°F). Top each burger with cheese slice during last minute of cooking.

4 Spread sour cream mixture over bottom halves of buns. Top with vegetables, burgers, guacamole, fire-roasted jalapeños and top halves of buns.

THE GREAT REUBEN SANDWICH
MAKES 2 SANDWICHES

4 slices rye bread

¼ cup Thousand Island dressing (see Tip)

8 ounces thinly sliced corned beef or pastrami

4 slices Swiss cheese

½ cup sauerkraut, well drained

2 tablespoons butter, melted

1 Spread one side of each bread slice with dressing. Top 2 bread slices with corned beef, cheese, sauerkraut and remaining bread slices.

2 Preheat air fryer to 330°F. Brush melted butter over bread. Cook sandwiches 3 to 5 minutes or until cheese is melted and bread is lightly browned and crispy. Serve immediately.

TIP
For a quick homemade Thousand Island dressing, combine 2 tablespoons mayonnaise, 2 tablespoons sweet pickle relish and 1 tablespoon cocktail sauce.

SOUTHWESTERN BLT

MAKES 2 SERVINGS

6 slices thick-cut applewood smoked bacon

¼ cup mayonnaise

1 teaspoon lime juice

¼ teaspoon ground chipotle pepper

¼ teaspoon ground cumin

1 large ripe tomato

2 pretzel rolls, split and toasted

½ cup shredded lettuce

1 Preheat air fryer to 390°F. Cook bacon 8 to 10 minutes; drain on paper-towel lined plate.

2 Combine mayonnaise, lime juice, chipotle pepper and cumin in small bowl; mix well.

3 Cut tomato into 4 thick slices. Spread cut sides of rolls with mayonnaise mixture. Top bottom halves of rolls with lettuce, tomato, bacon and top halves of rolls.

DINNER WINNERS

AIR-FRIED BEEF TAQUITOS

MAKES 6 SERVINGS

¾ pound ground beef

¼ cup chopped onion

1 tablespoon taco seasoning mix

6 corn tortillas

⅓ cup shredded Cheddar cheese, plus additional for topping

Salsa, sour cream and guacamole (optional)

1 Cook beef and onion in large skillet over medium-high heat 6 to 8 minutes or until browned, stirring to break up meat. Drain fat. Stir in taco seasoning.

2 Spoon about 2 tablespoons beef mixture in center of each tortilla. Top with about 1 tablespoon cheese. Roll up; secure with toothpicks. Spray with nonstick cooking spray.

3 Preheat air fryer to 370°F. Cook in single layer 3 to 4 minutes or until tortilla is browned and crispy.

4 Remove toothpicks before serving. Top with salsa, sour cream, guacamole and/or additional cheese.

SUBSTITUTION TIP

Try preparing taquitos with cooked chicken or pork and other types of cheese as well.

BANG-BANG CHICKEN ON RICE

MAKES 4 SERVINGS

CREAMY HOT SAUCE

- ½ cup mayonnaise
- ¼ cup sweet chili sauce
- 1½ teaspoons hot pepper sauce

CHICKEN

- ¾ cup panko bread crumbs
- ½ cup all-purpose flour
- 1 pound chicken breasts, cut into 1-inch pieces
- 2 green onions, chopped

  Hot cooked rice (optional)

1 Prepare Creamy Hot Sauce. Combine mayonnaise, chili sauce and hot pepper sauce in medium bowl. Divide mixture in half; set one half aside.

2 Place panko in shallow dish. Place flour in another shallow dish.

3 Using hands, toss chicken with flour until well coated. Dip chicken pieces in sauce mixture, then coat in panko. Spray with nonstick cooking spray.

4 Preheat air fryer to 390°F. Line basket with parchment paper.

5 Cook chicken in batches 10 to 12 minutes or until golden brown. Remove chicken to large plate; drizzle with remaining Creamy Hot Sauce.

6 Sprinkle with green onions. Serve over rice, if desired.

PARMESAN-CRUSTED CHICKEN

MAKES 4 TO 6 SERVINGS

4 to 6 boneless skinless chicken breasts (about 4 ounces each)

Salt and black pepper (optional)

1¼ cups Italian salad dressing

½ cup grated Parmesan cheese

½ cup finely shredded Provolone cheese

¼ cup buttermilk ranch salad dressing

4 tablespoons (½ stick) butter, melted

1 teaspoon minced garlic

¾ cup panko bread crumbs

1 Pound chicken to ½- to ¾-inch thickness between 2 sheets of waxed paper or plastic wrap with rolling pin or meat mallet. Season chicken with salt and pepper, if desired; place in large resealable food storage bag. Pour Italian dressing over chicken. Marinate in refrigerator at least 30 minutes.

2 Preheat air fryer to 370°F. Remove chicken from marinade. Cook 12 to 15 minutes, flipping halfway through cooking, until no longer pink in center and cooked throughout (165°F).

3 Combine Parmesan cheese, Provolone, ranch dressing, butter and garlic in large microwavable bowl. Microwave 30 seconds; stir. Add panko; mix to combine. Spread mixture over chicken.

4 Preheat air fryer to 390°F. Cook 2 to 3 minutes or until cheese is melted and topping is browned.

SERVING SUGGESTION

Serve with fresh steamed broccoli.

ZESTY ITALIAN CHICKEN NUGGETS
MAKES 4 SERVINGS

2 boneless skinless chicken breasts
¼ cup zesty Italian salad dressing
2 cloves garlic, minced
1½ teaspoons lime juice

1 tablespoon honey
½ teaspoon salt
¼ teaspoon black pepper

1 Cut chicken into 1-inch chunks. Place in large resealable food storage bag.

2 Combine dressing, garlic, lime juice, honey, salt and pepper in medium bowl. Pour over chicken; marinate in refrigerator 30 minutes to 1 hour.

3 Preheat air fryer to 370°F. Line basket with parchment paper. Remove chicken from marinade; discard marinade. Cook 10 to 12 minutes or until chicken is no longer pink and cooked throughout (165°F).

ISLAND FISH TACOS
MAKES 4 SERVINGS

COLESLAW

- 1 medium jicama (about 12 ounces), peeled and shredded
- 2 cups packaged coleslaw mix
- 3 tablespoons finely chopped fresh cilantro
- ¼ cup lime juice
- ¼ cup vegetable oil
- 3 tablespoons white vinegar
- 2 tablespoons mayonnaise
- 1 tablespoon honey
- 1 teaspoon salt

SALSA

- 2 medium fresh tomatoes, diced (about 2 cups)
- ½ cup finely chopped red onion
- ¼ cup finely chopped fresh cilantro
- 2 tablespoons lime juice
- 2 tablespoons minced jalapeño pepper
- 1 teaspoon salt

TACOS

- 1 to 1¼ pounds white fish such as tilapia or mahi mahi, cut into 3×1½-inch pieces
- Salt and black pepper
- 12 (6-inch) taco-size tortillas, heated
- Prepared guacamole (optional)

1 For coleslaw, combine jicama, coleslaw mix and 3 tablespoons cilantro in medium bowl. Whisk ¼ cup lime juice, ¼ cup oil, vinegar, mayonnaise, honey and 1 teaspoon salt in small bowl until well blended. Pour over vegetable mixture; stir to coat. Let stand at least 15 minutes for flavors to blend.

2 For salsa, place tomatoes in fine-mesh strainer; set in bowl or sink to drain 15 minutes. Remove to another medium bowl. Stir in onion, ¼ cup cilantro, 2 tablespoons lime juice, jalapeño pepper and 1 teaspoon salt; mix well.

3 For tacos, season both sides of fish with salt and black pepper. Preheat air fryer to 350°F. Spray basket with nonstick cooking spray. Cook fish in batches 8 to 10 minutes or until fish is opaque and begins to flake when tested with fork.

4 Break fish into bite-size pieces; serve in tortillas with coleslaw, salsa and guacamole, if desired.

PERI-PERI CHICKEN

MAKES 4 SERVINGS

1 small red onion, coarsely chopped

1 roasted red pepper (about 3 ounces)

¼ cup olive oil

¼ cup lemon juice

2 tablespoons white vinegar

4 cloves garlic, minced

1 tablespoon smoked paprika

1½ teaspoons salt

1½ teaspoons red pepper flakes

1 teaspoon dried oregano

½ teaspoon black pepper

1 cut-up whole chicken (3 to 4 pounds)

1 Combine onion, roasted pepper, oil, lemon juice, vinegar, garlic, smoked paprika, salt, red pepper flakes, oregano and black pepper in blender or food processor; blend until smooth. Remove half of marinade to small bowl; cover and refrigerate until ready to use.

2 Use sharp knife to make several slashes in each piece of chicken (about ¼ inch deep). Place chicken in large resealable food storage bag. Pour remaining marinade over chicken; seal bag and turn to coat, massaging marinade into chicken. Marinate chicken in refrigerator at least 4 hours or overnight, turning occasionally.

3 Remove chicken from refrigerator about 30 minutes before cooking. Preheat air fryer to 370°F. Line basket with foil.

4 Cook 20 to 25 minutes or until chicken is no longer pink in center and cooked throughout (165°F), brushing with some of reserved marinade every 15 minutes. Serve with remaining marinade, if desired.

MEATBALLS AND RICOTTA

MAKES 5 TO 6 SERVINGS (20 MEATBALLS)

MEATBALLS

- 2 tablespoons olive oil
- ½ cup plain dry bread crumbs
- ½ cup milk
- 1 cup finely chopped yellow onion
- 2 green onions, finely chopped
- ½ cup grated Romano cheese, plus additional for serving
- 2 eggs, beaten
- ¼ cup finely chopped fresh parsley
- ¼ cup finely chopped fresh basil
- 2 cloves garlic, minced
- 2 teaspoons salt
- ¼ teaspoon black pepper
- 1 pound ground beef
- 1 pound ground pork

SAUCE

- 2 tablespoons olive oil
- 2 tablespoons butter
- 1 cup finely chopped yellow onion
- 1 clove garlic, minced
- 1 can (28 ounces) whole Italian plum tomatoes, coarsely chopped, juice reserved
- 1 can (28 ounces) crushed tomatoes
- 1 teaspoon salt
- ¼ teaspoon black pepper
- ¼ cup finely chopped fresh basil, plus additional for garnish
- 1 to 1½ cups ricotta cheese

1 Preheat air fryer to 350°F. Brush 2 tablespoons oil over baking dish that fits into air fryer.

2 Combine bread crumbs and milk in large bowl; mix well. Add 1 cup yellow onion, green onions, ½ cup Romano cheese, eggs, parsley, ¼ cup basil, 2 cloves garlic, 2 teaspoons salt and ¼ teaspoon black pepper; mix well. Add beef and pork; mix gently but thoroughly until blended. Shape mixture by ¼ cupfuls into balls. Place meatballs on prepared baking dish; turn to coat with oil.

3 Cook 8 to 10 minutes or until meatballs are cooked throughout (160°F). Meanwhile, prepare sauce.

4 Heat 2 tablespoons oil and butter in large saucepan over medium heat until butter is melted. Add 1 cup yellow onion; cook 8 minutes or until tender and lightly browned, stirring frequently. Add 1 clove garlic; cook and stir 1 minute or until fragrant. Add plum tomatoes with juice, crushed tomatoes, 1 teaspoon salt and ¼ teaspoon black pepper; bring to a simmer. Reduce heat to medium-low; cook 20 minutes, stirring occasionally.

5 Stir ¼ cup basil into sauce. Add meatballs; heat 10 minutes, stirring occasionally. Transfer meatballs and sauce to serving dish; dollop tablespoonfuls of ricotta between meatballs. Garnish with additional Romano cheese and basil.

PARMESAN-CRUSTED TILAPIA

MAKES 6 SERVINGS

⅔ cup plus 2 tablespoons grated Parmesan cheese, divided

⅔ cup panko bread crumbs

⅓ cup prepared light Alfredo sauce (refrigerated or jarred)

1½ teaspoons dried parsley flakes

6 tilapia fillets (4 ounces each)

Shaved Parmesan cheese (optional)

Minced fresh parsley (optional)

1 Combine ⅔ cup grated Parmesan cheese and panko in medium bowl; mix well. Combine Alfredo sauce, remaining 2 tablespoons grated cheese and parsley flakes in small bowl; mix well. Spread Alfredo sauce mixture over top of fish, coating in thick even layer. Top with panko mixture, pressing in gently to adhere.

2 Preheat air fryer to 390°F. Line basket with foil or parchment paper; spray with nonstick cooking spray.

3 Cook in batches 8 to 10 minutes or until crust is golden brown and fish begins to flake when tested with fork. Garnish with shaved Parmesan cheese and fresh parsley.

BLACKENED CHICKEN TORTA

MAKES 4 SERVINGS

2 tablespoons vegetable oil

1½ tablespoons Creole seasoning

4 boneless skinless chicken breasts (about 4 ounces each)

½ cup sour cream

2 teaspoons lime juice, divided

½ teaspoon ground cumin

¼ teaspoon salt, divided
  Dash black pepper

⅓ cup mayonnaise

½ teaspoon chipotle chili powder

1 ripe avocado

4 slices (about 1 ounce each) Cheddar cheese

4 slices (about 1 ounce each) pepper Jack cheese

4 ciabatta rolls, split

1 cup finely shredded green cabbage or coleslaw mix

1 Combine oil and Creole seasoning in shallow dish; mix well. Add chicken; turn to coat completely with spice mixture. Let stand while preparing sauces.

2 Combine sour cream, 1½ teaspoons lime juice, cumin, ⅛ teaspoon salt and dash of pepper in medium bowl; mix well. Combine mayonnaise, remaining ½ teaspoon lime juice, ⅛ teaspoon salt and chipotle chili powder in small bowl; mix well. Mash avocado in another small bowl; season with additional salt and pepper.

3 Preheat air fryer to 370°F. Spray basket with nonstick cooking spray.

4 Cook chicken 12 to 15 minutes or until no longer pink in center and cooked throughout (165°F). Remove to plate; top each chicken breast with 1 slice Cheddar and 1 slice pepper Jack cheese. Tent loosely with foil to melt cheese.

5 For each sandwich, spread 2 tablespoons sour cream mixture on bottom half of roll; top with mashed avocado. Layer with ¼ cup cabbage and cheese-topped chicken breast. Spread heaping tablespoon mayonnaise mixture on top half of roll; close sandwich.

EGGPLANT PARMESAN

MAKES 4 SERVINGS

2 tablespoons olive oil

2 cloves garlic, minced

1 can (28 ounces) Italian whole tomatoes, undrained

½ cup water

1¼ teaspoons salt, divided

¼ teaspoon dried oregano

Pinch red pepper flakes

1 medium eggplant (about 1 pound)

⅓ cup all-purpose flour

Black pepper

⅔ cup milk

1 egg

1 cup Italian-seasoned dry bread crumbs

1 cup (4 ounces) shredded mozzarella cheese

Chopped fresh parsley (optional)

1 Heat oil in medium saucepan over medium heat. Add garlic; cook and stir 2 minutes or until softened (do not brown). Crush tomatoes with hands (in bowl or in can); add to saucepan with juices from can. Stir in water, 1 teaspoon salt, oregano and red pepper flakes; bring to a simmer. Reduce heat to medium-low; cook 45 minutes, stirring occasionally.

2 Meanwhile, prepare eggplant. Cut eggplant crosswise into ¼-inch slices. Combine flour, remaining ¼ teaspoon salt and black pepper in shallow dish. Beat milk and egg in another shallow dish. Place bread crumbs in third shallow dish.

3 Coat both sides of eggplant slices with flour mixture, shaking off excess. Dip in egg mixture, letting excess drip back into dish. Roll in bread crumbs to coat.

4 Preheat air fryer to 370°F. Spray basket with nonstick cooking spray. Cook in batches 10 to 12 minutes or until golden brown. Remove to plate; cover loosely with foil to keep warm.

5 Spray 9×9-inch* baking dish with cooking spray. Arrange eggplant slices overlapping in baking dish; top with half of warm marinara sauce. (Reserve remaining marinara sauce for pasta or another use.) Sprinkle with cheese.

6 Cook 1 to 2 minutes or just until cheese is melted and beginning to brown. Garnish with parsley.

If your air fryer is on the smaller side, you may need to use 2 smaller baking dishes.

FRENCH QUARTER STEAKS

MAKES 2 SERVINGS

½ cup water

2 tablespoons Worcestershire sauce

2 tablespoons soy sauce

1 tablespoon chili powder

3 cloves garlic, minced, divided

2 teaspoons paprika

1½ teaspoons ground red pepper

1¼ teaspoons black pepper, divided

1 teaspoon onion powder

2 top sirloin steaks (1-inch thick and about 6 ounces each)

3 tablespoons butter, divided

1 tablespoon olive oil

1 large onion, thinly sliced

8 ounces sliced mushrooms (white and shiitake or all white)

¼ teaspoon plus ⅛ teaspoon salt, divided

1 Combine water, Worcestershire sauce, soy sauce, chili powder, 2 cloves garlic, paprika, ground red pepper, 1 teaspoon black pepper and onion powder in small bowl; mix well. Place steaks in large resealable food storage bag; pour marinade over steaks. Seal bag; turn to coat. Marinate in refrigerator 1 to 3 hours.

2 Remove steaks from marinade 30 minutes before cooking; discard marinade and pat steaks dry with paper towel.

3 Heat 1 tablespoon butter and oil in large skillet over medium-high heat. Add onion; cook 5 minutes, stirring occasionally. Add mushrooms, ¼ teaspoon salt and remaining ¼ teaspoon black pepper; cook 10 minutes or until onion is golden brown and mushrooms are beginning to brown, stirring occasionally. Set aside. Combine remaining 2 tablespoons butter, 1 clove garlic and ⅛ teaspoon salt in small skillet; cook over medium-low heat 3 minutes or until garlic begins to sizzle.

4 Preheat air fryer to 390°F.

5 Cook steaks 10 to 15 minutes, flipping halfway through cooking, until desired doneness.* Brush both sides of steaks with garlic butter during last 2 minutes of cooking. Remove to plate and tent with foil; let rest 5 minutes. Serve steaks with onion and mushroom mixture.

Temperature for medium rare should be 135°F, medium 145°F, medium well 150°F.

BOURBON-MARINATED SALMON

MAKES 4 SERVINGS

¼ cup packed brown sugar

¼ cup bourbon

¼ cup soy sauce

2 tablespoons lime juice

1 tablespoon grated fresh ginger

1 tablespoon minced garlic

¼ teaspoon black pepper

4 salmon fillets (4 ounces each)

2 tablespoons minced green onion

1 Combine brown sugar, bourbon, soy sauce, lime juice, ginger, garlic and pepper in medium bowl; mix well. Reserve ¼ cup mixture for serving; set aside.

2 Place salmon in large resealable food storage bag. Pour remaining marinade over salmon; seal bag and turn to coat. Marinate in refrigerator 2 to 4 hours, turning occasionally.

3 Preheat air fryer to 390°F. Remove salmon from marinade; discard marinade.

4 Cook salmon 8 to 10 minutes or until fish begins to flake when tested with fork. Brush with reserved marinade mixture; sprinkle with green onion.

CHICKEN AIR-FRIED STEAK WITH CREAMY GRAVY

MAKES 4 TO 6 SERVINGS

½ cup all-purpose flour
½ teaspoon kosher salt
½ teaspoon onion powder
¼ teaspoon paprika
¼ teaspoon ground red pepper
⅛ teaspoon black pepper
1 large egg
¼ cup water
1 pound cube steak, divided into
    4 to 6 portions

GRAVY

1½ tablespoons butter
2 to 3 tablespoons all-purpose flour
¾ cup chicken broth
½ cup milk
    Salt and black pepper

1 Combine ½ cup flour, ½ teaspoon kosher salt, onion powder, paprika, ground red pepper and ⅛ teaspoon black pepper in shallow dish. Whisk egg and water in another shallow dish.

2 Dredge steaks in flour mixture, then egg mixture, letting excess drain back into dish, then again in flour mixture to coat well. Spray with nonstick cooking spray.

3 Preheat air fryer to 370°F. Spray basket with cooking spray or line with parchment paper sprayed with cooking spray.

4 Cook in batches 12 to 14 minutes, turning halfway through cooking, until steaks are browned and no longer pink in middle. Remove to serving plate.

5 For gravy, melt butter in small skillet over medium heat. Add 2 tablespoons flour, broth and milk. Cook and stir until slightly thickened. If necessary, add additional 1 tablespoon flour to thicken. Season with salt and black pepper. Serve steaks with gravy.

SPICY CRISPY SHRIMP

MAKES 4 SERVINGS

½ cup mayonnaise

4 teaspoons Thai chili sauce

1 teaspoon honey

½ teaspoon rice vinegar

¾ cup buttermilk

1 egg

¾ cup all-purpose flour

½ cup panko bread crumbs

1 teaspoon salt

½ teaspoon ground sage

½ teaspoon black pepper

¼ teaspoon onion powder

¼ teaspoon garlic powder

¼ teaspoon dried basil

16 large raw shrimp, peeled, deveined and patted dry

2 green onions, thinly sliced (optional)

1 For sauce, combine mayonnaise, chili sauce, honey and vinegar in small bowl; mix well. Cover and refrigerate until ready to serve.

2 Whisk buttermilk and egg in medium bowl until well blended. Combine flour, panko, salt, sage, pepper, onion powder, garlic powder and basil in separate medium bowl; mix well. Dip each shrimp in buttermilk mixture, then in flour mixture, turning to coat completely. Place breaded shrimp on large plate; refrigerate 15 minutes.

3 Preheat air fryer to 390°F; spray basket with nonstick cooking spray. Cook in batches 6 to 8 minutes or until golden brown, turning halfway through cooking. Remove to plate.

4 Transfer shrimp to large bowl; add sauce and toss gently to coat. Garnish with green onions.

RENEGADE STEAK ▸

MAKES 2 SERVINGS

1½ teaspoons coarse salt
½ teaspoon paprika
½ teaspoon black pepper
¼ teaspoon onion powder
¼ teaspoon garlic powder
⅛ teaspoon turmeric

⅛ teaspoon ground red pepper
⅛ teaspoon ground coriander
2 center-cut sirloin, strip or tri-tip steaks (1-inch thick and about 6 ounces each)
1 tablespoon butter

1 Combine salt, paprika, black pepper, onion powder, garlic powder, turmeric, ground red pepper and coriander in small bowl; mix well. Season both sides of steaks with spice mixture (you will not need all of it); let steaks stand at room temperature 45 minutes before cooking.

2 Preheat air fryer to 390°F. Cook 10 to 12 minutes, flipping halfway through cooking, until desired doneness.*

3 Brush steaks with butter; cook 30 seconds to 1 minute. Remove to plate; let steaks rest 5 minutes before serving.

Temperature for medium rare should be 135°F, medium 145°F, medium well 150°F.

TERIYAKI SALMON

MAKES 2 SERVINGS

¼ cup dark sesame oil
Juice of 1 lemon
¼ cup soy sauce
2 tablespoons packed brown sugar

1 clove garlic, minced
2 salmon fillets (about 4 ounces each)
Hot cooked rice
Toasted sesame seeds and green onions (optional)

1 Whisk oil, lemon juice, soy sauce, brown sugar and garlic in medium bowl. Place salmon in large resealable food storage bag; add marinade. Refrigerate at least 2 hours.

2 Preheat air fryer to 390°F. Spray basket with nonstick cooking spray.

3 Cook 8 to 10 minutes or until salmon is crispy and easily flakes when tested with fork. Serve with rice and garnish as desired.

PUB-STYLE FISH & CHIPS

MAKES 4 SERVINGS

¾ cup all-purpose flour, plus additional for dusting fish

½ cup flat beer

3 tablespoons vegetable oil, divided

2 large or 4 medium russet potatoes, peeled and cut into ½-inch-thick slices

¾ teaspoon salt, divided

¼ teaspoon black pepper

1 egg, separated

1 pound cod fillets

Prepared tartar sauce

Lemon wedges

1 Combine ¾ cup flour, beer and 1 tablespoon oil in small bowl; mix well. Cover and refrigerate 30 minutes up to 2 hours.

2 Toss potatoes with remaining 2 tablespoons oil. Sprinkle with ½ teaspoon salt and pepper. Preheat air fryer to 390°F. Cook potatoes 10 to 12 minutes, shaking occasionally during cooking, until crispy and browned. Remove to plate; keep warm.

3 Stir egg yolk into cold flour mixture. Beat egg white in medium bowl with electric mixer at medium-high speed until soft peaks form. Fold egg white into flour mixture. Season batter with remaining ¼ teaspoon salt.

4 Preheat air fryer to 390°F. Cut fish into pieces about 6 inches long and 2 to 3 inches wide. Dust fish with flour; dip fish into batter, shaking off excess. Cook 8 to 10 minutes, flipping halfway through cooking, until coating is browned and fish flakes easily when tested with fork.

5 Serve fish with potatoes, tartar sauce and lemon wedges.

STEAK FAJITAS

MAKES 2 SERVINGS

¼ cup lime juice

¼ cup soy sauce

2 tablespoons vegetable oil

2 tablespoons honey

2 tablespoons Worcestershire sauce

2 cloves garlic, minced

½ teaspoon ground red pepper

1 pound flank steak, skirt steak or top sirloin

1 medium yellow onion, halved and cut into ¼-inch slices

1 green bell pepper, cut into ¼-inch strips

1 red bell pepper, cut into ¼-inch strips

Flour tortillas, warmed

Lime wedges (optional)

Optional toppings: pico de gallo, guacamole, sour cream, shredded lettuce and shredded Cheddar-Jack cheese

1 Combine lime juice, soy sauce, oil, honey, Worcestershire sauce, garlic and ground red pepper in medium bowl; mix well. Remove ¼ cup marinade to large bowl. Place steak in large resealable food storage bag. Pour remaining marinade over steak; seal bag and turn to coat. Marinate in refrigerator at least 2 hours or overnight. Add onion and bell peppers to bowl with ¼ cup marinade; toss to coat. Cover and refrigerate until ready to use.

2 Remove steak from marinade; discard marinade and pat steak dry with paper towels. Preheat air fryer to 390°F. Spray basket with nonstick cooking spray. Cook steak 10 to 12 minutes, shaking occasionally, until desired doneness.* Remove to large cutting board; tent with foil and let stand 10 minutes.

3 Add vegetable mixture** to air fryer; cook 8 to 10 minutes or until vegetables are crisp-tender and beginning to brown in spots, shaking occasionally.

4 Cut steak into thin slices across the grain. Serve with vegetables, tortillas, lime wedges and desired toppings.

*Temperature for medium rare should be 135°F, medium 145°F, medium well 150°F.

**If your air fryer is on the smaller side, you may need to cut steak in half and cook steak and vegetables in batches.

COCONUT SHRIMP

MAKES 4 SERVINGS

DIPPING SAUCE

- ½ cup orange marmalade
- ⅓ cup Thai chili sauce
- 1 teaspoon prepared horseradish
- ½ teaspoon salt

SHRIMP

- 1 cup flat beer
- 1 cup all-purpose flour
- 2 cups sweetened flaked coconut, divided
- 2 tablespoons sugar
- 16 to 20 large raw shrimp, peeled and deveined (with tails on), patted dry

1 For dipping sauce, combine marmalade, chili sauce, horseradish and salt in small bowl; mix well. Cover and refrigerate until ready to serve.

2 For shrimp, whisk beer, flour, ½ cup coconut and sugar in large bowl until well blended. Place remaining 1½ cups coconut in medium bowl.

3 Preheat air fryer to 390°F. Line basket with parchment paper; spray with nonstick cooking spray.

4 Dip shrimp in beer batter, then in coconut, turning to coat completely. Cook in batches 6 to 8 minutes, turning halfway through cooking, until golden brown. Serve with dipping sauce.

ON THE SIDE

CRISPY BRUSSELS SPROUTS

MAKES 4 SERVINGS

1 pound Brussels sprouts, cut in half

1½ tablespoons olive oil

2 tablespoons grated Parmesan cheese

¼ cup ground almonds

1 tablespoon everything bagel seasoning or seasoning of your choice

1 Preheat air fryer to 370°F.

2 Toss Brussels sprouts, oil, Parmesan cheese, almonds and bagel seasoning in large bowl.

3 Cook 8 to 10 minutes, shaking occasionally during cooking, until Brussels sprouts are browned and crispy.

FRIED GREEN TOMATOES

MAKES 4 SERVINGS

⅓ cup all-purpose flour

¼ teaspoon salt

2 eggs

1 tablespoon water

½ cup panko bread crumbs

2 large green tomatoes, cut into ½-inch-thick slices

½ cup ranch dressing

1 tablespoon sriracha sauce

1 package (5 ounces) spring greens salad mix

¼ cup crumbled goat cheese

1 Combine flour and salt in shallow dish. Beat eggs and water in another shallow dish. Place panko in third shallow dish. Coat tomato slices with flour, shaking off excess. Dip in egg mixture, letting excess drip back into bowl. Roll in panko to coat. Place on plate.

2 Preheat air fryer to 370°F. Line basket with parchment paper.

3 Cook in batches 6 to 8 minutes or until golden brown.

4 Combine ranch dressing and sriracha in small bowl; mix well. Divide greens among 4 serving plates; top with tomatoes. Drizzle with dressing mixture; sprinkle with cheese.

POTATO SKINS

MAKES 3 SERVINGS

3 small baking or red skinned potatoes, baked*

1 tablespoon butter, melted

1 teaspoon salt

⅛ teaspoon black pepper

½ cup (2 ounces) shredded Cheddar cheese

3 slices bacon, crisp-cooked and coarsely chopped

¼ cup sour cream

1 tablespoon snipped fresh chives

Pierce potatoes with knife; bake in 425°F oven 45 minutes or in microwave on HIGH 5 minutes. Cool.

1 Cut potatoes in half lengthwise. Scoop out soft middles of potato leaving skins intact; reserve potato flesh for another use. Brush potato skins with butter; sprinkle with salt and pepper.

2 Preheat air fryer to 370°F.

3 Cook 5 to 6 minutes or until crisp. Top skins with cheese and bacon. Cook 3 to 5 minutes or until cheese is melted. Cool slightly. Top with sour cream and chives before serving.

GARLIC KNOTS

MAKES 20 KNOTS

4 tablespoons (½ stick) butter, divided

1 tablespoon olive oil

1 tablespoon minced garlic

½ teaspoon salt

¼ teaspoon garlic powder

1 package (about 11 ounces) refrigerated bread dough

½ cup grated Parmesan cheese

2 tablespoons chopped fresh parsley

½ teaspoon dried oregano

1 Melt 2 tablespoons butter in small saucepan over low heat. Add oil, garlic, salt and garlic powder; cook over very low heat 5 minutes. Pour into small bowl; set aside.

2 Roll out dough into 8×10-inch rectangle. Cut into 20 squares. Roll each piece into 8-inch rope; tie in a knot. Brush knots with garlic mixture.

3 Preheat air fryer to 370°F. Line basket with parchment paper.

4 Cook in batches 8 to 10 minutes or until knots are lightly browned. Meanwhile, melt remaining 2 tablespoons butter. Combine Parmesan cheese, parsley and oregano in small bowl; mix well. Brush melted butter over warm knots; immediately sprinkle with cheese mixture. Cool slightly; serve warm.

LOADED BAKED POTATOES

MAKES 4 SERVINGS

1 cup (4 ounces) shredded Cheddar cheese

1 cup (4 ounces) shredded Monterey Jack cheese

8 slices bacon, crisp-cooked*

4 medium baking potatoes, baked**

½ cup sour cream

¼ cup (½ stick) butter, melted

2 tablespoons milk

1 teaspoon salt

¼ teaspoon black pepper

1 tablespoon vegetable oil

2 teaspoons coarse salt

1 green onion, thinly sliced (optional)

*Cook bacon in preheated 390°F air fryer 6 to 8 minutes or until crispy. Remove to paper towel-lined plate. Cool completely.

**Pierce potatoes with knife; bake in 425°F oven 45 minutes or in microwave on HIGH 5 minutes. Cool.

1 Combine Cheddar and Monterey Jack in small bowl; reserve ¼ cup for garnish. Chop bacon; reserve ¼ cup for garnish.

2 Cut off thin slice from one long side of each potato. Scoop out centers of potatoes, leaving ¼-inch shell. Place flesh from 3 potatoes in medium bowl. (Reserve flesh from fourth potato for another use.) Add sour cream, butter, remaining 1¾ cups shredded cheese, bacon, milk, 1 teaspoon salt and pepper to bowl with potatoes; mash until well blended.

3 Turn potato shells over; brush bottoms and sides with oil. Sprinkle evenly with coarse salt. Turn right side up. Fill shells with mashed potato mixture, mounding over tops of shells. Sprinkle with reserved cheese and bacon.

4 Preheat air fryer to 370°F.

5 Cook 8 to 10 minutes or until filling is hot and cheese is melted. Garnish with green onion.

ZUCCHINI FRITTE

MAKES 4 SERVINGS

Lemon Aioli (recipe follows)

¾ to 1 cup soda water

½ cup all-purpose flour

¼ cup cornstarch

½ teaspoon coarse salt, plus additional for serving

¼ teaspoon garlic powder

¼ teaspoon dried oregano

¼ teaspoon black pepper

3 cups panko bread crumbs

1½ pounds medium zucchini (about 8 inches long), ends trimmed, cut lengthwise into ¼-inch-thick slices

¼ cup grated Parmesan or Romano cheese

Chopped fresh parsley

Lemon wedges

1 Prepare Lemon Aioli; cover and refrigerate until ready to use.

2 Pour ¾ cup soda water into large bowl. Combine flour, cornstarch, ½ teaspoon salt, garlic powder, oregano and pepper in medium bowl; mix well. Gradually whisk flour mixture into soda water just until blended. Add additional soda water, if necessary, to reach consistency of thin pancake batter. Place panko in shallow dish.

3 Working with one at a time, dip zucchini slices into batter to coat; let excess batter drip back into bowl. Coat with panko; pressing into zucchini slices to coat both sides completely.

4 Preheat air fryer to 390°F. Line basket with parchment paper.

5 Cook in batches 7 to 10 minutes or until golden brown. Sprinkle with Parmesan cheese and parsley. Serve with Lemon Aioli and lemon wedges.

LEMON AIOLI

Combine ½ cup mayonnaise, 2 tablespoons lemon juice, 1 tablespoon chopped fresh Italian parsley and 1 clove minced garlic in small bowl; mix well. Season with salt and pepper.

GARLIC AIR-FRIED FRIES

MAKES 4 SERVINGS

2 large potatoes, peeled and cut into matchstick strips

2 teaspoons plus 1 tablespoon olive oil, divided

1½ teaspoons minced garlic

½ teaspoon dried parsley flakes

½ teaspoon salt

¼ teaspoon ground black pepper

Ketchup, blue cheese or ranch dressing (optional)

1 Combine potato strips and 2 teaspoons oil in medium bowl; toss well.

2 Preheat air fryer to 390°F. Line basket with parchment paper.

3 Cook in batches 8 to 10 minutes, tossing occasionally, until golden brown and crispy.

4 While fries are cooking, combine remaining 1 tablespoon oil, garlic, parsley flakes, salt and pepper in small bowl.

5 Toss warm fries with garlic sauce. Serve immediately with ketchup, blue cheese or ranch dressing, if desired.

GREEN BEAN FRIES

MAKES 6 SERVINGS

DIPPING SAUCE

- ½ cup light mayonnaise
- ¼ cup light sour cream
- ¼ cup low-fat buttermilk
- ¼ cup minced peeled cucumber
- 1½ teaspoons lemon juice
- 1 clove garlic
- 1 teaspoon wasabi powder
- 1 teaspoon prepared horseradish
- ½ teaspoon dried dill weed
- ½ teaspoon dried parsley flakes
- ½ teaspoon salt
- ⅛ teaspoon ground red pepper

GREEN BEAN FRIES

- 8 ounces fresh green beans, trimmed
- ⅓ cup all-purpose flour
- ⅓ cup cornstarch
- ½ cup reduced-fat (2%) milk
- 1 egg
- ¾ cup plain dry bread crumbs
- 1 teaspoon salt
- ½ teaspoon onion powder
- ¼ teaspoon garlic powder

1 For dipping sauce, combine mayonnaise, sour cream, buttermilk, cucumber, lemon juice, garlic, wasabi powder, horseradish, dill weed, parsley flakes, salt and ground red pepper in blender; blend until smooth. Refrigerate until ready to use.

2 For green bean fries, bring large saucepan of salted water to a boil. Add green beans; cook 4 minutes or until crisp-tender. Drain and run under cold running water to stop cooking.

3 Combine flour and cornstarch in large bowl. Whisk milk and egg in another large bowl. Combine bread crumbs, salt, onion powder and garlic powder in shallow dish. Place green beans in flour mixture; toss to coat. Working in batches, coat beans with egg mixture, letting excess drain back into bowl. Roll green beans in bread crumb mixture to coat.

4 Preheat air fryer to 390°F. Cook in batches 6 to 8 minutes, shaking occasionally during cooking, until golden brown. Serve warm with dipping sauce.

HUSH PUPPIES ›

MAKES ABOUT 24 HUSH PUPPIES

1½ cups yellow cornmeal
½ cup all-purpose flour
2 teaspoons baking powder
¾ teaspoon salt

1 cup milk
1 small onion, minced
1 egg, lightly beaten
Ketchup (optional)

1 Combine cornmeal, flour, baking powder and salt in medium bowl; mix well. Add milk, onion and egg; stir until well blended. Let batter stand 5 to 10 minutes.

2 Preheat air fryer to 390°F. Line basket with parchment paper. Roll or drop batter by tablespoonfuls onto parchment-lined basket. Cook, in batches, 8 to 10 minutes or until golden brown. Serve hush puppies warm with ketchup, if desired.

BRUSSELS SPROUTS WITH HONEY BUTTER

MAKES 4 SERVINGS

6 slices thick-cut bacon, cut into ½-inch pieces
1½ pounds Brussels sprouts (about 24 medium), halved
¼ teaspoon salt

¼ teaspoon black pepper
2 tablespoons butter, softened
2 tablespoons honey

1 Preheat air fryer to 370°F. Cook bacon in medium skillet until almost crisp. Drain on paper towel-lined plate; set aside. Reserve 1 tablespoon drippings for cooking Brussels sprouts.

2 Drizzle Brussels sprouts with reserved bacon drippings and sprinkle with ¼ teaspoon salt and ¼ teaspoon pepper; toss to coat.

3 Cook 8 to 10 minutes or until Brussels sprouts are browned, shaking occasionally.

4 Combine butter and honey in medium bowl; mix well. Add Brussels sprouts; stir until completely coated. Stir in bacon; season with additional salt and pepper.

SIMPLE GOLDEN CORN BREAD

MAKES 9 TO 12 SERVINGS

1¼ cups all-purpose flour
¾ cup yellow cornmeal
⅓ cup sugar
2 teaspoons baking powder
1 teaspoon salt

1¼ cups whole milk
¼ cup (½ stick) butter, melted
1 egg
Honey Butter (recipe follows, optional)

1 Preheat air fryer to 370°F. Spray 8-inch square baking dish* with nonstick cooking spray.

2 Combine flour, cornmeal, sugar, baking powder and salt in large bowl; mix well. Beat milk, butter and egg in medium bowl until well blended. Add to flour mixture; stir just until dry ingredients are moistened. Pour batter into prepared baking dish.

3 Cook 12 to 15 minutes or until golden brown and toothpick inserted into center comes out clean. Prepare Honey Butter, if desired. Serve with corn bread.

*If your air fryer is on the smaller side, you may need to use 2 smaller baking dishes.

HONEY BUTTER

Beat 6 tablespoons (¾ stick) softened butter and
¼ cup honey in medium bowl with electric mixer at
medium-high speed until light and creamy.

SWEETS & TREATS

APPLE FRIES WITH CARAMEL SAUCE

MAKES 6 SERVINGS

½ cup all-purpose flour

2 large eggs

1 cup crushed graham cracker crumbs *or* 4 large graham crackers, finely crushed

¼ cup granulated sugar

2 medium Gala apples, cored and cut into 8 wedges each

CARAMEL SAUCE

½ cup packed brown sugar

¼ cup whipping cream

2 tablespoons butter

2 tablespoons corn syrup

¼ teaspoon salt

Vanilla ice cream (optional)

1 Place flour in small bowl. Beat eggs in shallow dish. Combine cracker crumbs with granulated sugar in another shallow dish.

2 Coat apple wedges in flour then in eggs, letting excess drip back into bowl. Coat with cracker crumb mixture; place on plate. Refrigerate 15 to 30 minutes.

3 Preheat air fryer to 390°F. Line basket with parchment paper. Cook apples 6 to 8 minutes or until slightly tender and golden brown.

4 Prepare Caramel Sauce. Combine brown sugar, cream, butter, corn syrup and salt in small saucepan. Heat over medium-low heat until warmed.

5 Serve apple fries with Caramel Sauce and/or ice cream, as desired.

CHOCOLATE CHUNK PIZZA COOKIE

MAKES 3 PIZZA COOKIES (2 TO 3 SERVINGS EACH)

2 cups all-purpose flour
1 teaspoon baking soda
1 teaspoon salt
¾ cup (1½ sticks) butter, softened
1 cup packed brown sugar
¼ cup granulated sugar

2 eggs
1 teaspoon vanilla
1 package (about 11 ounces) chocolate chunks
Vanilla ice cream

1 Preheat air fryer to 330°F. Spray 3 (6-inch) cast iron skillets, cake pans or deep-dish pizza pans with nonstick cooking spray.*

2 Combine flour, baking soda and salt in medium bowl; mix well. Beat butter, brown sugar and granulated sugar in large bowl with electric mixer at medium speed until creamy. Beat in eggs and vanilla until well blended. Gradually beat in flour mixture at low speed just until blended. Stir in chocolate chunks. Spread dough evenly in prepared pans.

3 Cook 12 to 14 minutes or until top and edges are deep golden brown but center is still slightly soft. Top with ice cream. Serve warm.

*If you don't have 3 skillets or pans, you can bake 1 cookie at a time. Refrigerate the dough between batches and make sure the skillet is completely cool before adding more dough. (Clean and spray the skillet again before adding each new batch.)

CHOCOLATE-ORANGE LAVA CAKES

MAKES 4 SERVINGS

Candied Orange Peel
(recipe follows, optional)
½ cup semi-sweet chocolate chips
¼ cup (½ stick) butter
½ cup powdered sugar,
    plus additional for garnish

2 eggs
2 egg yolks
¾ teaspoon orange extract
3 tablespoons all-purpose flour

1 Prepare Candied Orange Peel, if desired.

2 Combine chocolate chips and butter in microwave-safe dish. Microwave 45 seconds; stir until smooth. Whisk in ½ cup powdered sugar, eggs, egg yolks and orange extract. Fold in flour.

2 Preheat air fryer to 370°F. Spray 4 (4-ounce) ramekins with nonstick cooking spray. Pour batter into prepared ramekins.

3 Cook 10 to 12 minutes or until chocolate is set. Remove ramekins to wire rack; cool 15 minutes.

4 Run knife around edge of cake; remove to serving plate. Sprinkle with additional powdered sugar and garnish with Candied Orange Peel, if desired.

CANDIED ORANGE PEEL

MAKES ABOUT ½ POUND

3 large oranges
   Water

3 cups sugar, divided

1 Remove peel from oranges in strips; remove white membrane. Cut peel into ¼- to ½-inch-wide strips.

2 Place strips in heavy medium saucepan; cover with cold water. Bring to a boil over medium heat; drain and repeat 2 more times. Set aside orange peel.

3 Line baking sheet with waxed paper sprayed with nonstick cooking spray; set aside.

4 Combine ½ cup water and 1½ cups sugar in same saucepan. Cook over medium heat, stirring constantly, until sugar dissolves.

5 Add orange peel. Cook 10 to 15 minutes or until slightly translucent, stirring occasionally.

6 Place remaining 1½ cups sugar in shallow dish. Place orange peel in dish, a few strips at a time; toss to coat. Dry peel overnight on wire rack. Break into small pieces.

WARM APPLE CROSTATA

MAKES 4 TARTS (4 TO 8 SERVINGS)

- 1¾ cups all-purpose flour
- ⅓ cup granulated sugar
- ½ teaspoon plus ⅛ teaspoon salt, divided
- ¾ cup (1½ sticks) cold butter, cut into small pieces
- 3 tablespoons ice water
- 2 teaspoons vanilla
- 8 Pink Lady or Honeycrisp apples (about 1½ pounds), peeled and cut into ¼-inch slices

- ¼ cup packed brown sugar
- 1 tablespoon lemon juice
- 1 teaspoon ground cinnamon
- ⅛ teaspoon ground nutmeg
- 4 teaspoons butter, cut into very small pieces
- 1 egg, beaten
- 1 to 2 teaspoons coarse sugar
  Vanilla ice cream
  Caramel sauce or ice cream topping

1 Combine flour, granulated sugar and ½ teaspoon salt in food processor; process 5 seconds. Add ¾ cup cold butter; process 10 seconds or until mixture resembles coarse crumbs.

2 Combine ice water and vanilla in small bowl. With motor running, pour mixture through feed tube; process 12 seconds or until dough begins to come together. Shape dough into a disc; wrap with plastic wrap and refrigerate 30 minutes.

3 Meanwhile, combine apples, brown sugar, lemon juice, cinnamon, nutmeg and remaining ⅛ teaspoon salt in large bowl; toss to coat. Preheat air fryer to 370°F. Line basket with parchment paper.

4 Cut dough into 4 pieces; roll out each piece into 7-inch circle on floured surface. Place in prepared basket; mound apples in center of dough circles (about 1 cup apples for each crostata). Fold or roll up edges of dough towards center to create rim of crostata. Dot apples with 4 teaspoons butter. Brush dough with egg; sprinkle dough and apples with coarse sugar.

5 Cook in batches 12 to 14 minutes or until apples are tender and crust is golden brown. Serve warm topped with ice cream and caramel sauce.

FRUIT TARTS

MAKES 2 SERVINGS

1 refrigerated pie crust (half of a 15-ounce package)

1 tablespoon melted butter

¼ cup cherry, apple or blueberry pie filling

Coarse sugar

1 Unroll pie crust on clean work surface; cut into 4 pieces. Brush butter over dough. Spread pie filling over 2 pieces of dough; top each with second piece of dough. Seal edges by crimping with tines of fork. Brush tops with butter; sprinkle with sugar.

2 Preheat air fryer to 370°F. Line basket with parchment paper.

3 Cook 6 to 8 minutes or until light golden brown. Remove to plate; cool.

CHOCOLATE CHIP SKILLET COOKIE

1 cup plus 2 tablespoons all-purpose flour

½ teaspoon baking soda

½ teaspoon salt

6 tablespoons (¾ stick) butter, softened

⅓ cup packed brown sugar

¼ cup granulated sugar

1 egg

½ teaspoon vanilla

½ of a 12-ounce package semisweet chocolate chips

Sea salt (optional)

Ice cream (optional)

1 Preheat air fryer to 350°F. Spray 6- to 7-inch cast iron skillet with nonstick cooking spray.

2 Combine flour, baking soda and ½ teaspoon salt in medium bowl. Beat butter, brown sugar and granulated sugar in large bowl with electric mixer at medium speed until creamy. Beat in egg and vanilla until well blended. Gradually add flour mixture at low speed; beat just until blended. Stir in chocolate chips. Press batter evenly into prepared cast iron skillet. Sprinkle lightly with sea salt, if desired.

3 Cook 10 to 12 minutes or until top and edges are golden brown but cookie is still soft in center. Cool on wire rack 10 minutes before cutting into wedges. Serve warm with ice cream, if desired.

CINNAMON APPLES

MAKES 4 SERVINGS

¼ cup (½ stick) butter, melted

3 tart red apples such as Gala, Fuji or Honeycrisp (about 1½ pounds total), peeled and cut into ½-inch wedges

¼ cup packed brown sugar

1 teaspoon ground cinnamon

⅛ teaspoon ground nutmeg

⅛ teaspoon salt

1 tablespoon cornstarch

1 Combine melted butter and apples in 1½-quart baking dish;* stir well.

2 Add brown sugar, cinnamon, nutmeg and salt; stir until apples are glazed. Stir in cornstarch until well blended.

3 Preheat air fryer to 350°F. Cook 10 to 12 minutes or until apples are softened. Remove from air fryer; let stand 5 minutes for glaze to thicken. Stir again; serve immediately.

If your air fryer is on the smaller side, use a smaller baking dish or ramekins.

SWEETS & TREATS

INDEX

A

Air-Fried Beef Taquitos, 119
Air-Fried Parmesan Pickle Chips, 7
Almond Chicken Salad Sandwich, 104
Amazing Apple Salad, 62

Appetizers

Air-Fried Parmesan Pickle Chips, 7
Avocado Egg Rolls, 28
Bang-Bang Cauliflower, 14
Bruschetta, 8
Buffalo Cauliflower Bites, 20
Buffalo Wings, 36
Cheesy Garlic Bread, 34
Cinnamon-Sugar Sweet Potato Fries, 34
Crab Rangoon with Spicy Dipping Sauce, 40
Crab Shack Dip, 42
Crispy Mushrooms, 10
Macaroni and Cheese Bites, 16
Mediterranean Baked Feta, 38
Mini Egg Rolls, 44
Mozzarella Sticks, 26
Pepperoni Bread, 30
Pepperoni Stuffed Mushrooms, 22
Shanghai Chicken Wings, 24
The Big Onion, 18
Toasted Ravioli, 32
Zesty Lemon-Pepper Wings, 12
Apple Fries with Caramel Sauce, 175

Apples

Amazing Apple Salad, 62
Apple Fries with Caramel Sauce, 175
Autumn Harvest Salad, 74
Baked Apple Pancake, 50
Chicken Waldorf Salad, 72
Cinnamon Apples, 186

Warm Apple Crostata, 180
Autumn Harvest Salad, 74

Avocado

Avocado Egg Rolls, 28
Blackened Chicken Torta, 134
BLT Supreme, 102
Chicken and Avocado Overstuffed Quesadillas, 92
Guacamole Burgers, 112
Avocado Egg Rolls, 28

B

Baked Apple Pancake, 50
Bang-Bang Cauliflower, 14
Bang-Bang Chicken on Rice, 120
BBQ Chicken Salad, 68

Beef

Air-Fried Beef Taquitos, 119
Chicken Air-Fried Steak with Creamy Gravy, 142
Classic Patty Melts, 106
French Quarter Steaks, 138
Guacamole Burgers, 112
Meatballs and Ricotta, 130
Renegade Steak, 146
Steak Fajitas, 150
The Great Reuben Sandwich, 114
Blackened Chicken Torta, 134
BLT Supreme, 102
Bourbon-Marinated Salmon, 140

Breads

Cheddar Biscuits, 52
Cheesy Garlic Bread, 34
Garlic Knots, 160
Hush Puppies, 170
Pepperoni Bread, 30
Simple Golden Corn Bread, 172
Strawberry Banana French Toast, 56

Breakfast

Baked Apple Pancake, 50

Cheddar Biscuits, 52
Hearty Hash Brown Casserole, 48
Quick Jelly-Filled Biscuit Doughnut Balls, 54
Ricotta Pancakes, 47
Strawberry Banana French Toast, 56
Bruschetta, 8

Brussels Sprouts

Brussels Sprouts with Honey Butter, 170
Crispy Brussels Sprouts, 155
Roasted Brussels Sprouts Salad, 60
Brussels Sprouts with Honey Butter, 170
Buffalo Cauliflower Bites, 20
Buffalo Wings, 36

C

Cauliflower

Bang-Bang Cauliflower, 14
Buffalo Cauliflower Bites, 20
Cheddar Biscuits, 52
Cheesy Garlic Bread, 34

Chicken

Almond Chicken Salad Sandwich, 104
Amazing Apple Salad, 62
Autumn Harvest Salad, 74
BBQ Chicken Salad, 68
Bang-Bang Chicken on Rice, 120
Blackened Chicken Torta, 134
Buffalo Wings, 36
Chicken and Avocado Overstuffed Quesadillas, 92
Chicken and Roasted Tomato Panini, 110
Chicken Bacon Quesadillas, 108
Chicken Fajita Roll-Ups, 82
Chicken Parmesan Sliders, 100

Chicken Pesto Flatbreads, 98
Chicken Waldorf Salad, 72
Mediterranean Salad, 59
Nashville-Style Hot Chicken Sandwich, 80
Parmesan-Crusted Chicken, 122
Peri-Peri Chicken, 128
Seasoned Chicken Sandwich, 88
Shanghai Chicken Wings, 24
Strawberry Fields Salad, 66
Strawberry Poppy Seed Chicken Salad, 76
Superfood Kale Salad, 70
Zesty Italian Chicken Nuggets, 124
Zesty Lemon-Pepper Wings, 12
Chicken Air-Fried Steak with Creamy Gravy, 142
Chicken and Avocado Overstuffed Quesadillas, 92
Chicken and Roasted Tomato Panini, 110
Chicken Bacon Quesadillas, 108
Chicken Fajita Roll-Ups, 82
Chicken Parmesan Sliders, 100
Chicken Pesto Flatbreads, 98
Chicken Waldorf Salad, 72

Chocolate
Chocolate Chip Skillet Cookie, 184
Chocolate Chunk Pizza Cookie, 176
Chocolate-Orange Lava Cakes, 178
Chocolate Chip Skillet Cookie, 184
Chocolate Chunk Pizza Cookie, 176
Chocolate-Orange Lava Cakes, 178
Cinnamon Apples, 186
Cinnamon-Sugar Sweet Potato Fries, 34
Classic Patty Melts, 106
Coconut Shrimp, 152

Crab Rangoon with Spicy Dipping Sauce, 40
Crab Shack Dip, 42
Crispy Brussels Sprouts, 155
Crispy Mushrooms, 10
Cuban Pork Sandwich, 90

E
Eggplant Parmesan, 136

F
Fish & Seafood
Bourbon-Marinated Salmon, 140
Coconut Shrimp, 152
Crab Rangoon with Spicy Dipping Sauce, 40
Crab Shack Dip, 42
Island Fish Tacos, 126
Parmesan-Crusted Tilapia, 132
Pub-Style Fish & Chips, 148
Shrimp and Spinach Salad, 64
Spicy Crispy Shrimp, 144
Teriyaki Salmon, 146
Flatbread
Chicken Pesto Flatbreads, 98
Spinach Florentine Flatbread, 86
French Quarter Steaks, 138
Fried Green Tomatoes, 156
Fruit Tarts, 182

G
Garlic Air-Fried Fries, 166
Garlic Knots, 160
Green Bean Fries, 168
Guacamole Burgers, 112

H
Hearty Hash Brown Casserole, 48
Hearty Veggie Sandwich, 94
Hush Puppies, 170

I
Island Fish Tacos, 126

L
Loaded Baked Potatoes, 162

M
Macaroni and Cheese Bites, 16
Meatballs and Ricotta, 130
Meatless Meals
Eggplant Parmesan, 136
Hearty Veggie Sandwich, 94
Mushroom Po-Boys, 84
Spinach Florentine Flatbread, 86
Tuscan Portobello Melt, 79
Mediterranean Baked Feta, 38
Mediterranean Salad, 59
Mini Egg Rolls, 44
Mozzarella Sticks, 26
Mushroom Po-Boys, 84
Mushrooms
Crispy Mushrooms, 10
French Quarter Steaks, 138
Hearty Veggie Sandwich, 94
Mushroom Po-Boys, 84
Pepperoni Stuffed Mushrooms, 22
Tuscan Portobello Melt, 79

N
Nashville-Style Hot Chicken Sandwich, 80
New Orleans-Style Muffaletta, 96

P
Parmesan-Crusted Chicken, 122
Parmesan-Crusted Tilapia, 132
Pepperoni Bread, 30
Pepperoni Stuffed Mushrooms, 22
Peri-Peri Chicken, 128
Pork
BLT Supreme, 102
Brussels Sprouts with Honey Butter, 170
Chicken Bacon Quesadillas, 108
Cuban Pork Sandwich, 90
Loaded Baked Potatoes, 162

Meatballs and Ricotta, 130
Mini Egg Rolls, 44
New Orleans-Style
    Muffaletta, 96
Pepperoni Bread, 30
Pepperoni Stuffed
    Mushrooms, 22
Potato Skins, 158
Southwestern BLT, 116
Potato Skins, 158

Potatoes
Cinnamon-Sugar Sweet
    Potato Fries, 34
Garlic Air-Fried Fries, 166
Hearty Hash Brown
    Casserole, 48
Loaded Baked Potatoes, 162
Potato Skins, 158
Pub-Style Fish & Chips, 148
Pub-Style Fish & Chips, 148

Q
Quick Jelly-Filled Biscuit
    Doughnut Balls, 54

R
Renegade Steak, 146
Ricotta Pancakes, 47
Roasted Brussels Sprouts
    Salad, 60

S
Salads
Amazing Apple Salad, 62
Autumn Harvest Salad, 74
BBQ Chicken Salad, 68
Chicken Waldorf Salad, 72
Mediterranean Salad, 59
Roasted Brussels Sprouts
    Salad, 60
Shrimp and Spinach Salad,
    64
Strawberry Fields Salad, 66
Strawberry Poppy Seed
    Chicken Salad, 76
Superfood Kale Salad, 70

Sandwiches
Almond Chicken Salad
    Sandwich, 104
Blackened Chicken Torta, 134
BLT Supreme, 102
Chicken and Roasted
    Tomato Panini, 110
Chicken Parmesan Sliders,
    100
Classic Patty Melts, 106
Cuban Pork Sandwich, 90
Guacamole Burgers, 112
Hearty Veggie Sandwich, 94
Mushroom Po-Boys, 84
Nashville-Style Hot Chicken
    Sandwich, 80
New Orleans-Style
    Muffaletta, 96
Seasoned Chicken
    Sandwich, 88
Southwestern BLT, 116
The Great Reuben
    Sandwich, 114
Tuscan Portobello Melt, 79
Seasoned Chicken Sandwich,
    88
Shanghai Chicken Wings, 24
Shrimp and Spinach Salad, 64

Side Dishes
Brussels Sprouts with
    Honey Butter, 170
Crispy Brussels Sprouts, 155
Fried Green Tomatoes, 156
Garlic Air-Fried Fries, 166
Garlic Knots, 160
Green Bean Fries, 168
Hush Puppies, 170
Loaded Baked Potatoes,
    162
Potato Skins, 158
Simple Golden Corn Bread,
    172
Zucchini Fritte, 164
Simple Golden Corn Bread, 172
Southwestern BLT, 116
Spicy Crispy Shrimp, 144
Spinach Florentine Flatbread,
    86
Steak Fajitas, 150

Strawberries
Strawberry Banana French
    Toast, 56
Strawberry Fields Salad,
    66
Strawberry Poppy Seed
    Chicken Salad, 76
Strawberry Banana French
    Toast, 56
Strawberry Fields Salad, 66
Strawberry Poppy Seed
    Chicken Salad, 76
Superfood Kale Salad, 70

Sweets
Apple Fries with Caramel
    Sauce, 175
Chocolate Chip Skillet
    Cookie, 184
Chocolate Chunk Pizza
    Cookie, 176
Chocolate-Orange Lava
    Cakes, 178
Cinnamon Apples, 186
Fruit Tarts, 182
Warm Apple Crostata, 180

T
Teriyaki Salmon, 146
The Big Onion, 18
The Great Reuben Sandwich,
    114
Toasted Ravioli, 32

Tortillas
Air-Fried Beef Taquitos, 119
Chicken and Avocado
    Overstuffed Quesadillas,
    92
Chicken Bacon Quesadillas,
    108
Chicken Fajita Roll-Ups, 82
Island Fish Tacos, 126
Steak Fajitas, 150
Tuscan Portobello Melt, 79

W
Warm Apple Crostata, 180

Z
Zesty Italian Chicken
    Nuggets, 124
Zesty Lemon-Pepper Wings,
    12
Zucchini Fritte, 164

TRADEMARKS

Applebee's is a registered trademark of Applebee's Restaurants LLC.

Bahama Breeze is a registered trademark of Darden Concepts, Inc.

Bennigan's is a registered trademark of Bennigan's Grill & Tavern.

BJ's Restaurant & Brewhouse is a registered trademark of BJ's Restaurants, Inc.

Bonefish Grill is a registered trademark of Bonefish Grill, LLC.

Boston Market is a registered trademark of Boston Market Corporation.

Buca Di Beppo is a registered trademark of BUCA, Inc.

Buffalo Wild Wings is a registered trademark of Buffalo Wild Wings, Inc.

California Pizza Kitchen is a registered trademark of California Pizza Kitchen.

Carrabba's Italian Grill is a registered trademark of Bloomin' Brands, Inc.

Cheeseburger in Paradise is a registered trademark of Luby's Fuddruckers Restaurants LLC.

Chick-fil-A is a registered trademark of Chick-fil-A.

Chili's Grill & Bar is a registered trademark of Brinker International.

Corner Bakery is a registered trademark of CBC Restaurant Corp.

Cracker Barrel is a registered trademark of CBOCS Properties, Inc.

Dunkin' is a registered trademark of DD IP Holder LLC.

Earls is a registered trademark of Earls Restaurants Ltd.

El Pollo Loco is a registered trademark of El Pollo Loco.

Fazoli's is a registered trademark of Fazoli's System Management, LLC.

First Watch is a registered trademark of First Watch Restaurants, Inc.

IHOP is a registered trademark of IHOP Restaurants, LLC.

Jason's Deli is a registered trademark of DMI, Inc.

Joe's Crab Shack is a registered trademark of Landry's, Inc.

Legal Sea Foods is a registered trademark of Legal Sea Foods Restaurant Group Inc.

Legoland Parks and Hotels is a registered trademark of The LEGO Group.

Logan's Roadhouse is a registered trademark of SPB Hospitality Partners.

Longhorn Steakhouse is a registered trademark of Darden Concepts, Inc.

Maggiano's Little Italy is a registered trademark of Maggiano's Little Italy.

Marie Callender's is a registered trademark of Marie Callender's, Inc.

McDonald's is a registered trademark of McDonald's Corporation.

Nando's Peri-Peri Chicken is a registered trademark of Nando's.

Olive Garden is a registered trademark of Darden Concepts, Inc.

Outback Steakhouse is a registered trademark of Bloomin' Brands, Inc.

Panera Bread is a registered trademark of Panera Bread.

Pepe's Mexican Restaurants is a registered trademark of Pepe's Mexican Restaurants.

PF Chang's is a registered trademark of PF Chang's China Bistro, Inc.

Potbelly is a registered trademark of Potbelly Sandwich Works, LLC.

Red Lobster is a registered trademark of Red Lobster Hospitality, LLC.

Red Robin is a registered trademark of Red Robin International.

Ruby Tuesday, LLC is a registered trademark of Ruby Tuesday Operations LLC.

Ruth's Chris is a registered trademark of Ruth's Hospitality Group.

Soul Food Vegan is a registered trademark of Soul Food Vegan.

TGI Fridays is a registered trademark of TGI Fridays, Inc.

The Cheesecake Factory is a registered trademark of TFC Co, LLC.

The Original Pancake House is a registered trademark of Original Pancake House Franchising, Inc.

Tropical Smoothie Cafe is a registered trademark of Tropical Smoothie Cafe, LLC.

Which Wich? Superior Sandwiches is a registered trademark of Which Wich, Inc.

Wingstop is a registered trademark of Wingstop Restaurants, Inc.

Yard House is a registered trademark of Darden Concepts, Inc.

Zio's Italian Kitchen is a registered trademark of Zio's Italian Kitchen.

Zoës Kitchen is a registered trademark of Zoës Kitchen.

METRIC CONVERSION CHART

VOLUME MEASUREMENTS (dry)

$^1/_8$ teaspoon = 0.5 mL
$^1/_4$ teaspoon = 1 mL
$^1/_2$ teaspoon = 2 mL
$^3/_4$ teaspoon = 4 mL
1 teaspoon = 5 mL
1 tablespoon = 15 mL
2 tablespoons = 30 mL
$^1/_4$ cup = 60 mL
$^1/_3$ cup = 75 mL
$^1/_2$ cup = 125 mL
$^2/_3$ cup = 150 mL
$^3/_4$ cup = 175 mL
1 cup = 250 mL
2 cups = 1 pint = 500 mL
3 cups = 750 mL
4 cups = 1 quart = 1 L

VOLUME MEASUREMENTS (fluid)

1 fluid ounce (2 tablespoons) = 30 mL
4 fluid ounces ($^1/_2$ cup) = 125 mL
8 fluid ounces (1 cup) = 250 mL
12 fluid ounces (1$^1/_2$ cups) = 375 mL
16 fluid ounces (2 cups) = 500 mL

WEIGHTS (mass)

$^1/_2$ ounce = 15 g
1 ounce = 30 g
3 ounces = 90 g
4 ounces = 120 g
8 ounces = 225 g
10 ounces = 285 g
12 ounces = 360 g
16 ounces = 1 pound = 450 g

DIMENSIONS

$^1/_{16}$ inch = 2 mm
$^1/_8$ inch = 3 mm
$^1/_4$ inch = 6 mm
$^1/_2$ inch = 1.5 cm
$^3/_4$ inch = 2 cm
1 inch = 2.5 cm

OVEN TEMPERATURES

250°F = 120°C
275°F = 140°C
300°F = 150°C
325°F = 160°C
350°F = 180°C
375°F = 190°C
400°F = 200°C
425°F = 220°C
450°F = 230°C

BAKING PAN SIZES

Utensil	Size in Inches/Quarts	Metric Volume	Size in Centimeters
Baking or Cake Pan (square or rectangular)	8×8×2	2 L	20×20×5
	9×9×2	2.5 L	23×23×5
	12×8×2	3 L	30×20×5
	13×9×2	3.5 L	33×23×5
Loaf Pan	8×4×3	1.5 L	20×10×7
	9×5×3	2 L	23×13×7
Round Layer Cake Pan	8×1½	1.2 L	20×4
	9×1½	1.5 L	23×4
Pie Plate	8×1¼	750 mL	20×3
	9×1¼	1 L	23×3
Baking Dish or Casserole	1 quart	1 L	—
	1½ quart	1.5 L	—
	2 quart	2 L	—